101 PRAYERS TO HOLD ON TO

❦

W. PATRICK HARRIS

Edited by
KAREENA GRACIA-DESIR

KW Syndicate Publishing

Copyright © 2022 by W. Patrick Harris

All rights reserved.

No part of this book may be reproduced in any form or by any electronic or mechanical means, including information storage and retrieval systems, without written permission from the author, except for the use of brief quotations in a book review.

Contents

Preface	vii
Introduction	ix
1. Draw Me	1
2. The Unusual	3
3. The Combination	5
4. Nobody Knew	7
5. At The Finish	9
6. Blocked, Bound & Turned Around	11
7. Ask like Solomon	13
8. A Place to Land	15
9. The Reason	17
10. Take The Wheel	19
11. Journey to Bethlehem	21
12. Do Not Worry	23
13. I've Prayed Too Hard	25
14. The Remember The Tree Prayer	27
15. New Years Res-O-You-Tions	29
16. His Will	31
17. Matthew 6	33
18. The Game Changer	35
19. The Firmation	37
20. The Lie Detector	39
21. What A Game	41
22. The Prickly Promises	43
23. In The Middle	45
24. Practice	47
25. Gathered Then Gone	49
26. Knee Time	51
27. The Let Us Prayer	53
28. Divine Chain Reaction Prayer	55
29. The Flood	57
30. I Can Always Pray	59
31. The Hammer	61

32. The Sky is Falling	63
33. Data	65
34. Who do I Believe	67
35. Acceptance	69
36. While We Sleep	71
37. Midnight Shampoo	73
38. The Healing Shadow	76
39. Take Us Home	78
40. Sustain Us	80
41. Out With The Old	82
42. The Inside	84
43. Anytime, Anywhere	86
44. The Help Us Believe Prayer	88
45. The Open the Windows Prayers	90
46. The New Jerusalem Prayer	93
47. We Are Your Children	95
48. Call The Bank	97
49. Separation	99
50. A Change in the Atmosphere	102
51. The Referral	104
52. Out of Ashes	106
53. G-man	108
54. The Life or Death	110
55. Order Us	112
56. Incomplete	114
57. The Truth	116
58. More better	118
59. The Others	120
60. Should I	122
61. Be Glad	124
62. The Limitless	126
63. The Matchmaker	128
64. Accelerate	130
65. Claim the Promise	132
66. Brainstorm	134
67. Just a Sample	136
68. For Them	138
69. Right There	140
70. Better	142

71. If I hadn't	144
72. The Cruise Ship	146
73. Evidence	148
74. Just An Ounce	150
75. Not Goodbye	152
76. The Healing	154
77. Still Here	156
78. Never Stop Asking	158
79. Trust	160
80. Til The End	162
81. Birdly Confidence	164
82. The Children	166
83. The W.A.R.	168
84. No Wrong Numbers	170
85. The Hallelujah Pass	172
86. No Accident Prayer	174
87. Game Time	176
88. Do You Recognize?	178
89. Where There's Smoke	180
90. MIRACL1	182
91. Just Did It	184
92. Theories	186
93. Spoiled Rotten	188
94. What God?	190
95. In the News	192
96. Hammer	194
97. A.P.R.	196
98. The Lifted	198
99. Peace	200
100. Unspoken	202
101. Jesus Fuel	204
Afterword	207
Also by W. Patrick Harris	209

Preface

Welcome to the Hold On Family. To learn more about our outreach ministry, our other publications, and our products that you can wear and share with others, simply go to:

Holdon2overcome.com

Introduction

What is a prayer anyway? How does one pray? When? Why do people believe and what difference does it make? At the very least most people are hoping that there is something beyond themselves and searching for some kind of connection. People are naturally inquisitive and look for explanations, clarity, and the answers to their questions. We need to understand it all and we search to find out why we are even here, where we came from, and if there is a place beyond this time and space. Some may have been born into a family and raised to have a spiritual connection where others may have stumbled onto a faith based group as an adult. Maybe there was some life-altering event or near-death experience. But most often it is the hardships, the heartaches, the loneliness, the waiting, or the doubts that overwhelm the human faculties and cause us to question the very last remnants of whatever we believed. There is someone (maybe reading this right now) who wants to believe in something but there is a disconnect. There is a distance between what you have and what you hoped for, what you know and what you feel, your attempts at faith and the real challenges you are facing. The pressure has grown beyond those nursery rhyme prayers of

INTRODUCTION

"Now I lay me down to sleep" or "God is great and God is good, let us thank Him for our food."

You need to know. You need answers and results. You need direct feedback and empirical evidence if you're going to consider the idea that the words you speak create change. Be assured that you are *not* alone and that these messages are just for you. The fact that you are even reading this right now, at this moment in time is evidence that someone else has walked this path. These messages have a purpose. They are a testimony and remind us that our spoken words are heard. Even the utterances of our minds, our inner thoughts and hopes can be considered prayers and they do get through. It may not immediately change the situation but it will change you. It erases the feelings of helplessness and empowers a person. There is always something you can do to make a difference and you are never completely without options. Every day, in every situation and no matter the circumstance there is a chance for a change. In these pages we are sharing an inexhaustible source of hope in the form of conversations and that my friend is prayer.

I pray you are blessed.

Draw Me

Even as a youngster I was enthralled with archery. After quite a bit of begging and having to listen to many discussions about safety I was allowed to own a bow and a quiver of arrows. They were simplistic and yet at the same time so efficiently amazing. With the help of my father I set up an archery range with a target pinned to some bales of hay facing an open field in case an arrow missed the mark completely. I spent time practicing with that bow and arrows, squinting with one eye open while pulling the string and then releasing the arrows at the bullseye. Why did I love it so much? Was it the smooth, curved shape of the bow or the strength required to harness the force of it? Was it the power unleashed in virtual silence or the skill required to hit the desired target? Is it a stretch to imagine that sometimes our situations can make it seem like our lives, bodies and minds are one of those bows being pulled and stretched almost to the point of breaking? It's at those times that we need to realize that just like a bow and arrow, it's the pressure that produces the power. It's the pushing in one direction and pulling in the opposite direction that creates the energy. The bow and arrow can't be left in a relaxed state if you want to hit the bullseye. No, you have to stretch them maybe to the point of breaking to propel the arrows towards the intended target and goal. Sometimes we hit and sometimes we miss but remember it's the trial that produces the triumph. The test that leads to the testimony. It's a fact that a lot of pressure on a lump of coal produces a diamond. So sometimes we too have to be drawn to be released. Let's pray.

"*Dear Lord, we come now thankful to even be allowed to approach your throne. We thank you for all that we have and all that we are. For waking us and taking us through yet another day. For our food and for the life and health of our children. For the roofs over our heads and the shoes under our feet. We thank you for the knowledge that there is a God who put His plan in a book filled with promises we can Hold On to. Lord, we come individually and together believing that you hear us, will help us and answer all our prayers. Please show us our purpose today. Draw and then release us to the targets of breakthrough, healing and love. Should anything happen to us we ask that you forgive us and save us. In the name of Jesus, Amen.*"

Family, He promised us and He can not lie. If we keep praying and Holding On the outcome is sure. Today, is a great day, for the *release* of miracles.

PrayOn 2 Overcome. P2O.

The Unusual

What are you thankful for? Go a little deeper past the first few knee jerk reactions and cliches. Take a moment and look back, jot down a few things, then take a look at number seven on your list. What's the seventh thing you are thankful for? Delve past family, friends, food and a job. Usually the first few items on your list are the things you are glad about and/or things you could do for yourself. I propose that as you start really thinking and digging deeper into your own personal list you will find more than a few things that you know you did not and could not do for yourself. Some things can't be attributed to effort or even luck. The things you didn't see coming, the sickness you didn't know was there. Some things are truly unusual and it is the things that are beyond an explanation that require praise and thanksgiving. God is working and always waiting for us to give Him the credit for the miraculous things He has done.

"FATHER GOD, WE COME PRAISING YOU FOR EVERY WEEK, DAY AND hour of blessing. We can't count all the things but the fact that we are alive right now without pain is surely something to be thankful for. For holding the earth and sun at the perfect distance and not allowing these planets to crash together. For our family members, even the ones we

love from a distance. For the technology that allows us to communicate all around the world. For the people in our lives who cared enough to feed us and protect us. For the utilities, the clean running water and the luxury of having a bathroom with a toilet that flushes. Lord for all the times we pushed the brake pedal and the brakes worked. For all the stuff we've asked you for that we lost, threw away or don't even use anymore. Lord, we thank you for the million more blessings that we sometimes forget to mention and often times don't even realize we received.

Father, we thank you for the hope you give and the joy you bring. For reminding me that I am loved but not alone, healed but still a work in progress, not perfect but better than I was before. For Your word and it's assurance. For all the people that have prayed for me. Lord, for all the things I can not control I say thanks to you Jesus. Now I claim all the things that you promised for me, mine, and anybody else that prays with me. For those that are in need we pray for breakthroughs beyond measure. Please forgive me and save me, Amen."

See, if we think about it, there are a whole lot of *unusual* things to be thankful for. So give thanks and keep praying.

PrayOn 2 Overcome. P2O.

The Combination

Ok, for this one you may need to sit down, take a deep breath, and take a moment to let it sink in. Even if you aren't a numbers person this is going to make sense and I think you will be amazed. So here goes. When flipping a coin there are just two possible outcomes, heads or tails. The more times you flip the coin there will be more and more possible combinations of heads and tails. For example if someone asked you to pick any four random numbers you have a choice of all the numbers and all the different combinations of those numbers between 0000 and 9999. It's really spectacular to realize that just picking four random numbers will give you 10,000 different options and it's utterly mind-blowing to consider picking nine random numbers because that would mean picking numbers that are between 000000000 and 999999999. Nine random numbers will give you 1 BILLION different combinations. WOW! The more digits the more combinations.

So just try to imagine with all the people on the earth right now how many different combinations of prayers there are. Someone is praying for healing and a child while someone else is praying for a change in the weather. Someone needs a financial breakthrough and someone needs help making a decision. Somebody wants to relocate while someone else is looking for love while others just need fresh water. The lists of prayers are endless and therefore the combinations are endless. But now imagine that somewhere there is somebody in the same position that you are in, hoping for the same answer that you are hoping for. It may be a different language or dialect but you best believe you are not the only one that needs a breakthrough right now and so we have this prayer.

"FATHER, THANK YOU FOR THIS THING CALLED PRAYER AND THAT I AM not alone in it. I'm not the first nor will be the last person praying today but at this moment I come to lay my own particular combinations of cares at your feet along with all the others asking you Father to take them all and open the windows of heaven. You said in Romans 8 that we don't even know what to pray for but the Spirit Himself intercedes for us through wordless groans and so now I ask you to intercede for me. Please consider my hopes and dreams then bless me according to your will. Please look into the future and guide me around the pitfalls and towards the breakthroughs. For myself and all those in need please supply according to your riches. Father give me strength, courage, patience and peace. Finally I ask that you forgive me for not being perfect and help me to do better next time. In the name of Jesus I claim my blessing, Amen."

Just hold on and believe today that you are *not alone*. There are millions of people praying with you."

So PrayOn 2 Overcome. P2O

Nobody Knew

Three days ago a friend reported that someone had taken their own life. I just can't help but try to imagine what that person's last day was like. They must have felt alone. The tragedy of being alone, feeling alone and having nobody know it. Was the pressure that great, the pain that unbearable? Doesn't everybody have or know somebody, anybody at all that they can talk to? Somebody that will surely listen and understand? Somebody that won't judge or point fingers? Someone that won't give advice but instead will just be there when you need somebody to *just be there*? No? Well maybe sometimes talking isn't what's needed anyway. I know because I've been there. But there is somebody that is there for everybody whenever they just need anybody to be there for them. All it takes is a prayer.

"FATHER GOD WE COME REALIZING WE HAVE ALL HAD STRUGGLES AND there have been days where we didn't think we were going to make it through. Days when we didn't even want to make it through. Lord if we are honest we can admit that most of us have heard the voices encouraging us to throw in the towel, give up, just end it. And so we thank you for being there and protecting us from the attacks on our minds and spirits. Lord, we will never forget the angels you sent in the

form of people to say a kind word, offer a smile, or to just show they care. Thank you Lord for people like my friend Michelle who was intuitive enough to sense it, selfless enough to take the time and Christ-like enough to put her arms around me that day and pray for me when I was at my lowest.

Lord, we know the enemy is busy and seeks all day every day to take our very lives if he could and so we come now to bind and rebuke in the name of Jesus his methods of depression, anxiety, loneliness and the feelings of worthlessness. Lord, we ask you to shield us from heartache, mental illnesses, stress, separations and divorces. All the things that weigh us down like bullying, slander, shame and rejection. Father, we lift the young people burdened with abuse, neglect and hopelessness. Lord, we ask that you lift someone up right now out of darkness and despair. We pray that you reveal yourself right now and give them hope. Lord the finances are breaking someone and we ask you to send some money, pay the bill, reduce the debt and stop the calls to relieve the pressure. Someone's heart is broken again and we ask that you just let them be over it. Someone has heard the bad diagnosis so please send the results of the second opinion that reveals the healing. We pray that you come through for someone right now that is battling with and for life itself. Lord, show us the people that they need us to be there for them and give us the words, compassion, and conviction to not leave anyone who needs us to stay. We pray that because of our prayers and faithfulness no one we know will be able to say I was hurting and nobody knew or cared. Use us Lord to touch and save lives. We offer this prayer and our service for your honor and glory, Amen."

Hold on Family, today is a great day for a breakthrough. Maybe it's the day we can be the breakthrough for someone else who needs us to be there for them. We don't have to look any further than the people we already know. Determine not to let this day end without reaching out to offer an ear, a shoulder or a hand that someone else can Hold On to.

HELP THEM 2 OVERCOME. HOLD THEM 2 OVERCOME. HT2O

At The Finish

I had to share this. I saw this story, and it just... moved me. To see the same story of Kyla Montgomery you can look up the youtube clip entitled "Young Athlete Pushes the Limits of a Crippling Disease" https://bit.ly/2I6cdTE

To think it, believe it and *hold on* all at the same time can be a daunting task sometimes. I am imagining Jesus as my own personal coach just standing there waiting for me at the finish line and cheering me on knowing that by the time I get to Him I just might not be able to stand on my own any longer. The race that you are running may be taking every ounce of energy, effort and faith you can muster but the key to victory is to just keep going. Ecclesiastes 9:11 says, "The race is not given to the swift or to the strong. But to the one that endures to the end." You win a race one step at a time, picking them up and putting them down knowing each stride is bringing you closer to victory. It's at those times you literally can't stop to pray or do anything fancy. There will be times when all you can do is think it out loud.

. . .

*"FATHER GOD, THANK YOU FOR BEING MY COACH. THANK YOU FOR sight, hearing and limbs that move at all. I'm not complaining about running this race because I know that there are plenty of people that have never even taken a single step at all and so I lift those with far bigger challenges than I have. Father please bless those that wouldn't give in to cancer and didn't give up on friends and family, those that are fighting through addictions and those who are caring for someone that can't care for themselves. Father there are those who don't have enough and some who can't see their way through, those who are doing it for love and those who are praying you send them the one to love. Lord, we pray for all those giving it their all today and ask that you remind them what will happen if they just keep running with their eyes on you. Show them what you've prepared for those who keep going. Encourage them with the fact that there **is** an end, a breakthrough, a finish line where you are waiting for them with open arms. I claim the blessings for your honor and glory. In the mighty name of Jesus, Amen."*

I Corinthians. 9:24 tells us to "run in such a way as to get the prize" because today, is a great day, to reach the finish line.

HoldOn 2 Overcome. H2O.

Blocked, Bound & Turned Around

I had three people within 24 hours ask me to pray for their children and grandchildren. Understanding how hard the enemy works to bring death and destruction to our children I prayed with each person right then and there that the attack from the enemy on these young lives would be *blocked, bound* and *turned around*. God sent angels to protect baby Moses floating down the river in a basket made of reeds. God sent angels to protect and relocate baby Jesus to safety in Egypt. God has a special place in His heart for our children and so I'm sharing again right now this same prayer for you, your children or someone you may know who needs the help of angels, with their own little angels.

"FATHER GOD, FOR THE LIFE, HEALTH, AND STRENGTH OF OUR children again I say thank you. The only love greater than our love for our children is Your love for us. We know that even though we try our best we just can't protect them from everything all the time. Lord, we know that we cannot always be there to save them and so we step forward in faith asking you Lord to cover them. Father, we know the enemy is jealous because we can create life and he targets even our help-

less babies and so we lift pregnant and delivering mothers. We know he attacks toddlers and so we pray for the patience and kindness of caretakers as well as their parents and children. We know he tries so hard to get the attention of our teenagers and so we pray for their families and friends. Lord we know that schools can be targets and dangerous places and so we request angels to protect against all violence or attacks outside and inside. We ask for protections from drugs, alcohol, peer pressure and the wrong crowd. We lift all the teachers, administrators, and support staff. Father, when will our children ever be too big for us to love or worry about and so ask for blessings over our adult children as well. We especially lift families dealing with special needs children and all the other challenges families may face.

Father, we declare in the mighty name of Jesus that the enemy will not have his way nor come near our children without having to fight past legions of armed and Holy angels. We pray that you shield them from every attack with the wings of your heavenly warriors. We claim the promise of your word that if we will be faithful and train up our children in the way they should go that they will not depart from it. Lord, we pray any and all negativity aimed at our children will be blocked, bound and turned around. We are your children praying for our children in the name of Jesus, Amen."

Hold On family, we know that in our past somebody prayed and covered us so that we could be here today. So now we pray for ours and the next generations to come. Keep lifting them and they *will* overcome.

HoldOn 2 Overcome. H2O

Ask like Solomon

What is it that you are praying for? In 1 Kings 3 and 2 Chronicles 1 it is recorded that the Lord God Himself appeared to Solomon and asked him "What shall I give thee?" Who wouldn't love to be in those shoes? Who wouldn't want to be asked that by the One that created everything, has everything and can create more of anything. What do you want? *Nothing* you'd say would be impossible and *everything* you say would appear. Wow, that would be wonderful wouldn't it? Well, Hold On Family, aren't we praying to that same great God? Isn't He still capable of anything? So today we too can ask like Solomon.

"FATHER GOD, WE COME TO THANK YOU FOR ALL THE BLESSINGS. THE blessings that were seen, unseen, forgotten and some we just overlooked. We know we have received what we never asked for, we have been carried when we couldn't walk and we were protected when we couldn't see. We know that you have already blessed us far more than we deserve and because of what you have done we come even more confident that what we need today isn't too much to ask. We come asking you to shape us like Solomon to make wise choices. Guide us like Solomon to not be selfish. Bless us like Solomon beyond material things but with health, long life and prosperity in what you give us to do. Lord, we need you to cleanse our hearts and minds so that we aren't

obsessed, greedy and mesmerized by what we want. We know that true happiness and fulfillment will only come by resting in your will and so we surrender to you. Like Solomon we offer ourselves in service. For your good, your glory and in the name of Jesus, Amen."

Hold On, and ask for anything. He will answer.

JUST HOLD ON, HOLDON 2 OVERCOME. H20

A Place to Land Prayer

Imagine what it was like for Noah's family. This small band of humans had been through quite an ordeal while trying to survive at a time even God Himself said that He regretted creating human beings. Years of begging and preaching to people that only criticized him while he worked tirelessly building this massive boat completely by hand. They had all seen the animals march in formation to the ark and then go inside and still the people were unconvinced. After being sealed inside the storms begin and they feel the ark move, sway and ride the currents as the rains came down and the floods came up. Then above the sounds of the tumultuous storm they hear the anguished cries of those outside, maybe friends and family as they pleaded for their lives. These eight people spend hundreds of days confined inside this floating barn with beasts great and small with no idea what was happening to their world outside. They've endured it all and finally the boat comes to rest. A short time later they see a ray of sunshine through a window at the top of their houseboat but still they are confined and can't get out or go on with a normal life. They are still stuck unable to move forward or forget. So they wait for a sign, the fulfillment of the promise, the final breakthrough. Sound familiar? Noah sends out a raven that brings back no good news. Then a dove that returns with no good news. Two birds, two separate attempts, try and try again.....sound familiar? The birds fly around looking for hope, relief, a sign that they are finally free of their captivity. Flying and flying with no place to land. Some days, I just need to land.

"FATHER GOD, WE THANK YOU FOR ALL THE ARKS YOU'VE PROVIDED for us and the storms seen and unseen that you have taken us through. We are still standing, praying and holding on. Some of us have had to face storms and have been confined in unpleasant circumstances but we held on to our faith. Things have changed all around us, nothing is the same, and our familiar places don't even exist anymore. Now we are searching, looking for signs and listening for answers. So we come to you Jehovah who sees and knows all things asking you to guide and direct us to the resting place. For our failures and shortcomings we ask for your forgiveness. Now just like Noah and his family we come today claiming the promises for a renewed life after death and destruction. Lord, for the praise and honor we will give you. For the others to be blessed by our testimonies because we are your children asking in the mighty name of Jesus. Please show us our place to land. Amen."

In Genesis 8:11, a dove brings back an olive leaf. Then seven days later Noah released a dove that didn't return at all because it had found that place to land.

HOLD ON. HOLDON 2 LAND. H2O

The Reason

I f God brought me here, if He is keeping me here then there *must* be a reason. For everything there is a time, a place, a season and a reason. Look for and then focus on that reason. Believe and Hold On to the reason.

"FATHER, I THANK YOU. THIS MORNING I HAVE ALREADY HEARD *reports of death and disease. This morning I saw a terrible accident and ambulances responding. This morning I know that people woke up outdoors, hungry and without warm clothes but Father, although I am such a mess you still saw fit somehow to shelter, feed and clothe me and so I say thank you. I believe you are keeping me for Your reasons and so I ask that you reveal them to myself and those praying with me today. I pray someone looks at their children and realizes that they are a blessing and a reason to keep going. Please open lines of communication between spouses so they see each other as a reason to keep working on their relationship. I pray somebody goes to work today and takes the opportunity to comfort someone and then realize the real reason for their job is not just for the paycheck but for the lives that can be touched and changed for the better. Father, I pray that we do not ignore the person on the street today or the person with the sign asking for help. Help us to realize that all these encounters are with people that need us and that is the reason you placed us there at that time.*

Lord, for the doctors and nurses you send us to witness to. For the lawyers, judges and people at the courthouse. For the neighbors, teachers and people at the gym. For the delivery person, whoever, wherever we go today let us see the reason so we'll know that our living is not in vain. In the mighty name of Jesus we ask it, Amen."

H2O Family, do you believe that there is a reason for you being where you are today? Some of those reasons call us mommy or daddy and some call us friends. Although we may never know or meet most of them in this lifetime let's Hold On knowing that our lives caused a ripple effect. We touch people that touch people and so on. Try to focus on that today. Let's confirm it together. "God has a time, a place, a season and a reason for me [say your name]" Today and every day is a new opportunity to find out what it is.

HOLD ON FOR IT. HOLDON 2 OVERCOME.

Take The Wheel

You might have heard the saying, "Let go and let God." Quite catchy and it sounds easy enough but to really put it into practice we have to first learn to do that first part, let go. In theory once we've prayed about it and done our best we should supposedly be able to just let go and let God but we are human and humans often have a difficult time with submission and control. We like control, want control, need control. So saying "let go and let God" can be far easier than actually *letting go and letting God*. If you need help with it today, try these words.

"FATHER GOD WE COME RIGHT NOW TO THANK YOU FOR ALL THE *times, places and situations that it was You who brought us through. All the times you saved me even from myself. For all the times you took the wheel so that I can still be alive today, thank you Father and now Father I am asking You to help me to let it go. I need more faith, Lord. I'm still like a child afraid to let go but worse because I'm an adult and I am supposed to have conquered some fear by now. Lord, You said to take action, be diligent, to work like the ant and not be lazy but help me to understand when you want me to move forward and when you want me to be still, and wait. I don't want to make a bigger mess of my situation so I need to know which way to go? I'm asking you first Lord. I'm putting you first Lord like you asked me to do. I don't want it to be by my power but by Yours so today Lord I give you permission to take the wheel. Not out of my hands but out of the car altogether so I won't be tempted to reach for it again or steer in my own direction.*

Father, I admit that I don't know where I'm going anyway. I need You to help me live by faith so that I can be confident in your God-omatic pilot to navigate my way. Please give me peace while trusting in you. This is my prayer of submission, acknowledging that you are the one true and living God. In the name of Jesus I let it go, Amen."

H2O Family, it's not easy but with practice we can learn to rely on God's driving skills. He promised so let's keep praying because sometimes we have to let go, to Hold On.

HoldOn 2 Overcome. H2O.

Journey to Bethlehem

Everyone has contemplated the age old question of why am I here and then we realize that the "here," the unordinary places, the unusual circumstances and those crazy situations are often just what God uses to reposition us. He looks into the future then arranges to put us in the right place at the right time to intersect with the blessing. If it feels like you are on a long, uncomfortable journey just imagine Mary as it is written in Luke 2:4-5 and what she might have been thinking while slowly traveling down that dusty road leading to Bethlehem. She has been given some information but no details. Some instructions but no playbook. What was she thinking? What words did she pray?

"FATHER GOD, WE COME TO YOU TODAY TO SAY THANK YOU AND admit our inability to see what you see. Lord, we humans need an omnipotent and omniscient God and that's why we believe, worship and pray to you. Some of us find ourselves in strange places and we need some extra faith to keep going. We didn't plan for our lives to be this way. We never thought that following your directions would take us away from our homes and families. Like Mary we accepted your instruction and still we find ourselves on a slow ride across a barren desert. Fortunately Lord we have your Word and so we know about Mary's amazing outcome. We know her journey led her towards the

wise men that were looking for her and the gifts she needed for the child to come. Lord please put us on the path that will lead us to our Bethlehem Breakthroughs as well.

Lord, we bring you everything that we are unsure of and we ask that you give us strength as you bring us to the place where Your promises will be brought to life. I can't see it Lord but I believe you know when and where everything will come together. In the name of Jesus I claim it, Amen."

It was truly a great leap of faith for Mary and Joseph to make that first trip but the Bible records in Matthew 2 that soon after the birth of Baby Jesus they had to take another journey to Egypt and then another journey back to Nazareth. Hold On Family, are you ready to travel? It's the road to Bethlehem that prepares you for the next journey and we won't stop until we make it home.

HoldOn 2 Overcome. H2O.

Do Not Worry

Some people may consider reading God's word confusing. They often report that certain versions of the Bible are hard to read or understand but even if you don't have a full grasp on the prophecies of Daniel, the 2300 days or the 3 angels message there are some things that are so clear, so direct, so simple that anyone can grasp them. For example, everyone knows the meaning of the words *do not*, right? Do not means stop. Whatever words come after do not, you aren't supposed to do that. So when God commands *do not* which is pretty simple, what should be our reaction? OK, so then why are you worrying? Matthew 6:25 says, "Therefore I tell you, do not worry." Matthew 6:31, says it again, "So do not worry." Then in Matt 6:34 it says "Therefore do not worry." Oh, there's more. Matt 10:19, Mark 23:11, Luke 12:11, Luke 12:22, and 29, and 21:14 all repeat the same 3 words. It covers from what you eat to what you wear and even what to say. God tells us to "do not worry about tomorrow or even your life." Hold on family, God said it over and over again. Do not worry. Why is it repeated so many times? How can He just say that and expect it to happen so easily? Because He has it all in the control of His hands and He knows how it's going to end. So take your worrying and give it to Him.

. . .

"LORD JESUS, THANK YOU FOR YOUR WORDS THAT SPEAK DIRECTLY TO my situation. Jesus, I can not fix it, handle it or stop thinking about it. Therefore God I ask you to please take it from me, strengthen my faith and give me peace. Lord, please take this worrying from me. I give it all to you. For all you've done, for what you are doing, and for what you promised you will do when I ask in your name. Thank you Jesus, Amen."

It is pretty simple isn't it? Hold on and *do not* worry. Give it to Him to worry about and then just HoldOn 2 Overcome! H2O

I've Prayed Too Hard

Someone said "Yes," then they said "No." Someone said a call would come and then no call came. Someone said meet me at noon and then they didn't show up. Someone said they would be there for you and then they were nowhere to be found. People often aren't dependable and many times things don't go as we planned but I've prayed too hard to be discouraged. I've prayed too hard to lose faith now. I just have to believe that even these things, the no's, the rejections and disappointments are *still* a part of His plan. I've come too far now to not believe that once it has been lifted in prayer, it is in His hands and "all things work together for good." Speaking or even thinking those words lightens my load by taking the burden out of my hands and placing it in His care and so the outcome will be His will. We only have to speak the words.

"FATHER GOD, WE ARE GATHERING NOW TO APPROACH YOUR PLACE and space called prayer. We are coming to your throne and we say thank you as we take our places at your feet. We want to believe that all this stuff, the changes, challenges, the ups and downs are all a part of your plan. It seems that sometimes it is one thing after the other and despite all our hopes and efforts we can not reach our goal. We do get tired, we do get weary and doubt does creep in. There are days when

our fear battles with our faith and we aren't sure who's winning. Lord, are we being ungrateful to ask if we will ever be happy and will it ever go as we had planned?

Lord, we've done what you asked and that's all we can do. Please lift us up as we wait for your answers. We don't want to be worried or timid so grant us the courage to hold our heads up and chests out as we march forward into tomorrow believing that if the call doesn't come, if they aren't the one, if it takes a while longer then that's OK because we've prayed too hard to question your answers. Lord you promised us and repeated in your Word that you would prosper and heal us so if it hasn't happened yet we will just believe it is only a matter of time. If we are going to believe anything at all we choose to believe in you rather than the disappointments. Therefore we will rest on the assurance that it is settled, ordained and arranged for our favor and the blessings are on the way. Amen."

Hold On Family it's true that we all do get weary. God knows our struggles and He wants to help us. Sometimes it may take a little time and that is when we have to Hold On. Just remember, once you've prayed about it you can let it go. Repeat these words for a reminder- "Tag, you're it Jesus. I give the worry and the burdens to you. I've prayed too hard to carry *it* any longer."

Now all you have to do is Hold On.

HoldOn and Overcome. H2O

The Remember The Tree Prayer

I was driving in a residential neighborhood and noticed what had apparently been a Christmas tree that was laying on the curb at the end of someone's driveway. Imagine that only a few days ago this now discarded tree was the center of attraction. A day or so ago it was elevated, decorated and celebrated. Now it's stripped, discarded, unloved and thrown out for garbage. A rejected tree but this isn't the first time people rejected a tree, is it?

"FATHER GOD, WE COME TO YOU TODAY SO THANKFUL THAT WE EVEN have homes and for the ability to celebrate a holiday. We want to first remember those around this world that are homeless or seeking shelter. We know there are people that were in situations that led them to run away from home and we ask you to bless them. Lord, we know there are far too many children today that are like this tree, left outside, alone and rejected. Please provide for them and protect them like only you can.

Lord, we realize that we have rejected you. We want things and we have no problem asking you to help us get them. We beg and pray to get our way. We may even fast, make promises and commit to New Year's

Resolutions but our minds are still fixed on the earthly things we desire more than the One who is the provider. We make a big deal about getting the tree. We admittedly want the gifts to be under the tree. We accept the presents and the celebrations around the tree and then Lord we so easily forget the one who blessed us with the tree in the first place.

Father, how many times have we taken you for granted by forgetting about the tree you carried for us and were nailed to? Actually, we don't even speak much about it after the holiday season has passed. Time moves on and we forget about the star, the baby, the message and the sacrifice. So today I pray that someone reading this right now will be reminded of what You did for them, on a tree, at Calvary. Let today be the day someone decides to give their life to you because of what You gave for them. Thank you for being willing to take our place and die for us, in order to forgive and save us, Amen."

It was settled on a tree that they made into a cross, so that I could be free.

HOLDON 2 OVERCOME. H2O

New Years Res-O-You-Tions

There is a growing movement today even amongst the family of believers that is gradually replacing Christ with "I." It seems Philippians 4:13 has been edited to state "I can do all things….," period. They read the first five words and stop the text right there. Church leaders can be heard stimulating their audiences with, "I can do all things…get that house." Or, "I can do all things… get that luxury car you've been wanting." Quoting the scripture in this way translates to "I can do all things, through I." But aren't they leaving a part out, the most important part out?

Oh sure, hard work and determination sounds good and rather innocent on the surface. But let us not forget that none of our accomplishments, the degrees earned, the social media followers, or the number of countries visited are by our own efforts. Proverbs 19:21 makes it plain for us today, "Many are the plans in a person's heart, but it is the *Lord's purpose that prevails.*" Phillipians 4:13 actually says, "I can do all things, *through Christ* who strengthens me." It's the Christ in I, and not the "I" in Christ. So even if it is not January 1st New Years day, today is a great day to make a change and decide to put God *first*. Only He sees the end from the beginning and brings it all to pass. Psalms 37:5 instructs us to submit everything to Him and He will bring it to pass. Let's ask Him to help us replace "I" with "You."

"*Dear Jesus, I come to give you the credit, the honor and the praise. Lord it was You who gave me life then showed me grace and mercy to save that life over and over again. I know I didn't keep my heart beating through the night and I didn't wake myself up this morning. I'm coming to you realizing how easy it has been to get caught up in the day to day routine that I don't spend enough time with You. I know I have been distracted. I can't help but want the nice things I see Lord but please help me to not become so mesmerized that I forget about You. So I'm coming now to ask You, to seek You, to inquire of You and to put You first in my life. In your Word you showed us how the perfect man, the strongest man and the wisest man all fell. The greatest warrior and the richest man all failed when they got arrogant and had too much success. So if these men couldn't do it on their own I know that I don't stand a chance without your wisdom to guide my path. Starting today I want you to chose the way I should go and please speak your instructions clearly so I will know it is You.*

Father, I ask that anyone seeing, reading, or receiving this prayer whenever it may be will determine in their heart to make a resoY-OUtion. Lord, help us to pray first, ask first, seek your will first and then have faith that you will handle all the rest. You are the potter and I am the clay so take this life and shape it for your purpose and allow us to claim all the blessings that come with being obedient to you. In the mighty name of Jesus we pray not our will, but thy will be done, Amen."

Hold on Family, God gave each of us a purpose but how will you know if you never really ask Him what it is and spend all your time going after what you want? Ask Him, put Him first, and then Hold On for all the things He will accomplish through you for His glory.

HoldOn 2 Overcome. H2O

His Will

HIS
WILL

If we prayed and I mean really prayed about it then we can be sure that no matter what the situation looks like right now the outcome is and will surely be His Will. If God is in control and God is most definitely in control then what is happening right now must be His will. If I believe and I am honestly trying to believe then I must accept that whatever transpires today will be His design. Whatever happened is just what was supposed to have happened in order for it to work out for my good because He said it would. So I just have to keep telling myself over and over that this, even this, is His will. It's His will, His will, His will. No matter what. It is HIS will. For a better understanding we only have to talk to Him about it.

"DEAR LORD, THANK YOU FOR ORDERING MY STEPS AND SINCE I can't take credit for it and I know there's not that much luck in the world, I'm going to say thank You Lord. Now today, whether it's blue skies or cloudy storms please help me to see Your will in it. I come now to pray a revelation prayer and ask that you do for us what you did in Numbers 22 for Balaam and his donkey. Please open our eyes. I am asking you Father to help us to understand so that we can better Hold On. What could be better to ask for than to understand you Lord? I'm

not even asking to make it easier necessarily, but I am asking for the encouragement of knowing it's all for a reason. Yes Lord, encourage me, reinforce me, strengthen me and affirm me in Your will. Please forgive and save me. I ask this in the mighty and powerful name of Jesus, Amen."

Whoever is reading this know that you are not alone. I too sometimes have to wonder and repeat it to myself. It's His will, His will, His will. The more we reinforce it in our minds the better we will be able to understand and accept the outcomes. Hold On because today is a great day for that *breakthrough*.

So HoldOn 2 Overcome. H2O

Matthew 6

I just happened upon this scene and snapped this picture as it reminded me of Matthew 6. "*Don't worry,*" it says and then that very same message is repeated five times. Now look at those little black birds literally lined up to take their turn passing through that puddle for their bath and their blessing. Do you think they are worrying? The bills, the kids, the job, that impossible situation? I seriously doubt it because they know the one who made that promise in Matthew 6.

"*F*ATHER, IT'S ONLY FITTING TO SAY THANK YOU, HALLELUJAH AND *praise the Lord because I made it! Thank you for my sight that allowed me to see those birds. I pray for all those without sight, hearing, and those suffering with all forms of health challenges. I come to pray to you your very own words that you gave me in Matthew 6 which tells me to not even worry about life itself. Father, I thank you for my life, food, water and shelter. If you've kept all these needs met then I know you are capable of doing it again today. Please supply all my needs according to your riches. Lord, I thank you for your reminders you place in the most obvious places including those birds. I know they don't have jobs, bank accounts or benefit packages but I still see them* *getting the things they need day by day which then reminds me that your Word is true.*

I admit that I have worried and you were right, it surely did not add a single hour to my life. I do see the flowers and know that they don't work or make clothes but they surely are dressed in beauty. So your Word does make sense and comes to life whenever I look around. Lord, I have to believe that if you care that much for the plants and the animals then you must care for me, your child, made in your image and called by your own name. Jesus, if I believe you loved me enough to die for me then I must also believe that you will take care of me. So I'm going to try to not worry about food, water, or clothes because even the people who don't claim to believe have those things. Instead of worrying I'm going to choose to praise you in all my situations and Hold On. Because today is a great day for my breakthrough. In the name of Jesus I claim it all and more abundantly. Amen."

Read it for yourself in Matthew 6:25-34 and claim it. Anytime you need a reminder, look for some birds. "His eye is on the sparrow and I know He watches me."

HOLDON 2 OVERCOME. H2O.

The Game Changer

Somewhere someone wakes up with a pain that cannot be ignored and then finds out that the pain was a sign of cancer. People get up every morning feeling fine then have a stroke, heart attack or a brain aneurysm. Someone smells smoke in their house and then barely escapes with their life from a destroying fire. Who has ever gone to work and the doors are locked or they walk in to learn about layoffs and budget cuts? There is no doubt that the game of life can be very unpredictable and after these moments life may never be the same again but Hold On, the game may change but there is still time on the clock. Hold On, you still have all your timeouts. Hold On, your coach is undefeated in the finals. There are game changing events but there are also Game Changing Prayers.

"GOD, NO MATTER WHAT THE SITUATION YOU ARE STILL GOD AND YOU *are still good and so we just thank you again for all that you've done. We have faced and are facing some serious situations and we need you right now to send some angels on our behalf. There are many people in hospitals so we pray for healing today and ask that someone open their eyes, someone gets out of bed and someone goes home as a witness to your ability to perform miracles. Lord, we know that as long as life is in their bodies, you can change the game in their favor and so we ask you to do just that. We pray for more than healing but complete restoration of minds and bodies. We pray today that some doctors will shake their heads and have no choice but to acknowledge they have witnessed miracles. We ask because we know you are the game changer.*

Lord, someone has a short time to pay their bills. Someone needs an answer. Someone is praying for loved ones. Lord, whatever the situation I pray right now that if things went wrong in one moment that in less than a moment you will change the game, fix the problem and defeat the enemy on their behalf. We claim the game changing examples in your word of Joseph who went from the jail to the palace and David who in one day went from Shepherd to being King. The account of Naaman who in one hour went from diseased to restored and Lazarus who from sleeping in the grave to walking from the tomb. So we claim these same breakthroughs for our situations and lives today because we believe in you Father, the one and only true and living God. Please forgive us and save us in the name of Jesus we pray, Amen."

Family, I feel a little more inspired now. I *know* what He can do in an instant. I've read it. I've seen it and I've lived it and so I declare that our God is a Game Changer! So Hold On for it because today, is a great day, for that instantaneous change.

HoldOn 2 Overcome. H2O.

The Firmation

Two words that are often interchanged are **Affirm**ation and **Confirm**ation. Even the definitions seem to be synonymous. An Affirmation is "to state as fact, declare one's support for, to uphold strongly and firmly" and Confirmation is "to establish the truth or correctness of, to state with assurance something is true, establish validity." Well have you ever needed, asked for, waited for, hoped for...a **firmation**? You didn't care if it was a grammatically correct **confirm**ation or **affirm**ation. You just needed to know could I, should I, will I, which way do I go? Well today, we are going to ask for and claim that "firmation."

"FATHER GOD, HERE WE ARE AGAIN TODAY WITH SOME HOPE BECAUSE of what you've already done for us in the past. For the answers and guidance, for the closed doors and open windows and all the safekeeping we just want to say thank you. Lord for those of us that believe we are in control of our lives please be merciful and let us be reminded that we did not keep the blood flowing while we sleep at night so there has to be something greater than ourselves. So we come now needing a word from the Living Word. Lord, while many may think they have it figured out I admit without hesitation that I do not know and so I need a firmation today. I am at a fork in the road and I need to know which

way to go? I am contemplating choices today and I need you to show me which one? There are people in my life and I need to know who should stay and who should go? About this crazy job Lord should I quit or keep on trying to be a witness? There is an offer on the table, should I take it or wait a while longer? They gave a diagnosis and a prognosis but Jesus what do you recommend for my healing? Lord should I invest or divest, invert or divert? Lord I know you can see the future so should I move on or hold on because I need to overcome?

I have asked and I believe you will answer. Until then I will wait for the phone call, the letter in the mail or however you choose to speak to me today. In the name of Jesus I claim your affirmation, your confirmation and your blessings, Amen."

Let's continually pray for each other. You thought you were the only one struggling with decisions? No brothers and sisters, you are not alone. We are all in need of answers and we have come to the right place because today, is a great day, to receive the answer.

So Hold. HoldOn 2 Overcome. H2O

The Lie Detector Prayer

W ould you feel comfortable taking a lie detector test if they asked these questions? How much time do you spend reading the Bible? Do you really believe in God? Do you think Jesus is real and He is coming back one day soon? Hmmm. What if they asked are you sure that prayer works? Are you tired of praying the same prayer that hasn't been answered? Those could be some uncomfortable questions to consider let alone answering them knowing that someone can tell if you are telling the truth or not. Most people may not like to be put on the spot with that kind of questioning but maybe we need to be just that honest with ourselves and God.

"FATHER, WE BEGIN AGAIN WITH SAYING THANK YOU. IF FOR NOTHING else we want to give you credit for all the unexplainable miracles in our daily lives. Lord, some of us are OK and don't need to ask for anything in particular and then there are some of us that have been praying and fasting, and hoping and Holding for a long time. Lord, we want to believe that it's better on our knees. We want to give praises and share testimonies but you Lord, who sees and knows everything, you know a

lot of people are just faking it, getting by and smiling to keep from crying. Many people surely would not take that lie detector test. So we come now to put down our pretenses and strained smiles. We come to lay it all out there in the open, let it all go and cry out to you to please help us Father. The world is going mad all around us and we need to know what to do and which way we should go?

Lord, how many people live double lives while trying to hide addiction, affairs, sickness and of course unhappiness, and all-out skepticism about all this God stuff? Today we are not faking or playing when we say we need You and we need you to come through today. Let us feel your presence and power. Let there be a difference in the life of anyone praying and all who read this message. Just the fact that we are still praying is evidence of the mustard seed faith you said in your word could move mountains and so in the name of Jesus I claim mountains be moved. Father, you are the only one that we can turn to so please let today be the day we see our God answer our prayers. Amen."

Family, sometimes we have to just be *REAL* and lay it out there. You don't have to pretend with our Savior. You can tell Him how you really feel. He won't be offended and He won't turn away. He knows what and how you feel anyway and He cares. Our enemy is the father of all lies and so we can defeat him with the truth that we speak. So keep praying and Hold On. Today, is a great day, for the truth to be revealed.

HoldOn 2 Overcome. H2O

What a Game

More than a decade ago the Houston Astros played in the World Series but were crushed, humiliated and spanked like school children in a four game sweep. For a decade they were remembered as the defeated team. They had not had a single winning season or a chance for the championship. However it's a team effort. Every player is necessary from the offense, defense, runners, catchers, pitchers and hitters and in the game of life champions don't give up. Maybe that's why today after years of preparation, thousands of hours of practice, blood, sweat and tears the Houston Astros are World Champions. With persistence, they won the World Series and with persistence we too will be more than conquerors.

"FATHER GOD, FOR THE HEALTH AND STRENGTH WE GIVE THANKS right now. We come Lord asking first for blessings upon every man, woman and child that has never thrown a ball and may never run a base until they get to glory. Now Father we come to claim the promise of your Word and ask you to coach us today to victory. Lord, if I can be a pinch-encourager, then put me in the path of someone that needs their spirits lifted and their hope restored. Lord, if I have to sacrifice to bring another home, then give me strength to Hold On until it's my turn.

Lord, this game is long with a lot of extra innings and we are tired and weary. We were ahead and winning and then we were behind and losing but Lord we still believe that if you are on our side all things are possible and the game isn't over until you say it's over and so we press on.

Lord, there were some obvious calls that didn't go our way. There were some unexpected setbacks and unforced errors that could cost us the game. Father, we admit that we stood still and watched hittable opportunities go by and then we foolishly swung at temptations way out of our strike zone. So here we are today facing challenges on the mound that have a daunting record of striking people out but we pray today that our opposition to happiness in all forms will be retired and sent packing. Father, we know we can because You can. You brought us this far so please make us champions. Not for trophies but for the witness we will give, the lives we will touch and the praise we will offer to you, the only true and living God. We claim the victory in the name of Jesus, Amen."

Today is a great day for me to become a champion. Think it's not, just ask a Houston Astros. Hold On to your bat, step up to the plate and swing for the fences. Say it with me, "Victory *is* mine."

HOLDON 2 OVERCOME. H2O.

The Prickly Promises

They are called hazelnuts and there are several different varieties. The one in the picture here is the prickly kind and let me tell you those little thorns H-U-R-T. It's like no matter how you try to pick one up, your fingers are going to get pricked and then it burns. It's actually a nut that grows and then falls off the tree while it's still green and the shell is completely enclosed inside the husk of sharp quills. Much like the blessings and breakthroughs we pray and Hold On for. Fortunately over time the nut's covering begins to dry out and shrink. After that the covering splits open. A little more time and the outer layer which was blocking access to what's inside, shrinks even more until it reveals what's desired. The prize is still in the hard shell but at least you can pick it up without getting stabbed by those needle sharp little quills. Now you can break away the last covering and feast on the promises that were so well hidden inside. The prize, the nutrients, the reward are all on the inside waiting to be revealed.

"FATHER GOD, FOR THE LESSONS OF LIFE YOU TEACH US THROUGH *nature we say thank you. Lord, we come now on this day to present our prickly lives, situations, loved ones, minds and bodies. Lord, we believe* and are yet holding on for our due season when the thorns and spurs will shrink back and we will finally be able to hold the smooth, delicious promise in our hands and rejoice to reap the harvest that will nourish our souls. We know Lord that it won't be because we are righteous but because we are still here trying. Not because we are complete, but because we refuse to complain. Not because we are perfect, but because of Your promise.

So we have picked up Your Word even when it pricked us and we have turned its pages even when we didn't know what we were looking for. We dug in beneath the surface looking for some source of life and now we repeat back to you Lord the words of Jeremiah that said there will be a reward for our labor. The sticks and pricks will pay off. The stings will release the sweet meat of blessings. Lord, from what we hold in our hands we declare in all our lives that this is a time for breakthroughs. Lord God please protect us, our children and families and show us the way. So in the mighty name of Jesus I yet again claim it and promise to give no praise to anything or anybody but you Jehovah. For any and everyone who reads and so is covered by this prayer we thank you now for the answers we will receive in the name of Jesus, Amen."

Hold on, keep praying even if they are Prickly Prayers because today is a great day, for what's inside to break through.

HoldOn 2 Overcome. H2O.

The In The Middle Prayer

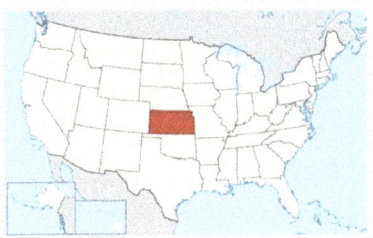

The news today is apocalyptic. Right now there are people on one coast fighting the flames of wildfires while people on the other coast are fighting the ravages of flood waters. Fires in the West. Too much water in the East and then an earthquake just took place somewhere in the middle. If not for the grace of God there could be a strong Eastward wind blowing those flames Eastward, and a strong Westward current pushing the water Westward until they actually meet *in the middle* having destroyed everything in their path across the entire country. But Hold On Family, this isn't the first time we have seen natural disasters. If we read Exodus 14 we will be reminded that there was another situation with a raging river on one side and a pillar of fire on the other and yet that day was a mighty day of breakthrough for those in the middle that believed in their God.

"FATHER GOD, THANK YOU FOR THIS WORD THAT WE CAN LOOK TO for the encouragement we need. For your guiding, safekeeping, grace and mercy we say thank you. We come today from all kinds of different places but with the common connection that we all need something bigger and greater than ourselves. Through storm and rain, sickness

and pain you have protected us and kept us safe in the middle. Father, some may say luck but we say Lord. Those who have lived just long enough to have seen some fires and lived through some floods and all manner of things no one can explain, we know there is a God who sits high and reaches low and so we come today to present ourselves helpless and hopeless to control the forces of nature but believing that you have it all in your hands. Father, we need you to put out the fires and push back the floods. Father we know that when you speak to the wind and rain they obey so please Lord rebuke the negative and prosper the positive in our lives today.

Lord, we are waiting on you and none other. Someone needs the job and the money while someone needs the healing and rest. Someone is praying for their children and many need their relationships to be fixed. There are those needing food and shelter while others are praying to lose weight and sell a property. From the most basic of necessities to the wildest possible dreams we come to you Father for your blessings. We need to know which way to go Lord or if we should go at all. Please hear our prayer and give us strength while we wait here in the middle. In the name of Jesus we claim our blessings, Amen."

A map of the United States reveals that the middle is somewhere in Kansas but where we want to be is safe in the middle of our creator's arms. I declare that today is a great day for a miracle. So no matter what's happening around us, on either side, above or beneath, just keep trusting and hold on.

HoldOn 2 Overcome. H2O.

Practice

Sometimes we all need practice, at everything, even giving praise. Those days and we all have them, when life itself can be challenging to say the least. The Word is filled with the writings of the shepherd who later became King David. From his boyhood days herding flocks to the days he lived as the feared warrior and King, he wrote quite extensively about challenges and giving praises, the highs he experienced when defeating enemies and the lows realizing his own potential for self-destruction. It is at the end of his poetic Song of Psalms in chapter 150 that we find King David giving his famous tutorial on giving praise. Over and over again he offers to God his Praise. Thirteen times David speaks the word, "Praise." David, having served as the exorcist and banisher of the demons that tormented King Saul knew well the power of praise in the war against evil. Remember these words. Write them down and never forget this secret to defeating the enemy. *The devil can't stand in the presence of God's praise.* Praise defeats the enemy. Praise reminds the enemy of his future. I believe it's no accident that God wanted us to have Psalms 150. So today let's practice our praise.

. . .

"*Father God, we come again to say Thank You. No matter what our situation may be, we're going to approach this throne of yours today with thanksgiving. We thank you for hearts that beat and lungs that expand; for air to breath and eyes that see; for those of us who can't see as clearly we will give thanks for the privilege of having glasses. We know right now there are people going into surgery to fix hearts and bodies. We know there are those that are blind and are still praying for a miracle to restore their sight. Father, we will always give thanks knowing there is somebody on the opposite side of what we are giving praise for. We have food, but somebody is hungry. We have friends and family but somebody else is alone. Thank you for freedom when some are not free. Thank you for the ability to move about and even if it's not fancy we have transportation to get us places we want to go. Lord for those who don't have cars we are thankful that we still have legs to get us to where we need to go. We are grateful for brains that still operate while so many have Dementia or Alzheimers and can't remember at all. For a safe place to lay our heads when whole countries have been devastated and so many homes have been destroyed by fires, floods and wars. Thank you for clothes that may be old but at least we can put on something. For 10 fingers, and 10 toes, a mouth, some ears, a working nose. Father, we are practicing our praise and have only just begun to touch the surface with what you've done on our behalf.*

The more we give praise the better we see Your hands at work in and over our lives. We know the things we've hoped for and the things we've been blessed with. Sometimes it was even better than we could have imagined. We can try but we know that only you have the potential to supply every possible need and fix every broken heart. Only You can see us through all possible dilemmas and escort us safely to the breakthrough. Lord today we practice so tomorrow we can shout and dance like David danced. Please take it all Father and we will be sure to give you all the credit for what we couldn't do ourselves. In the name of Jesus we offer our practice and our praise, Amen."

Let's keep *practicing* today and see if we can't get the attention of heaven. Practice your praise and Hold On.

HoldOn 2 Overcome. H2O.

Gathered Then Gone

We drove by this house and couldn't help but notice that there were all these buzzards hanging around. They were sitting on the roof, on the lawn, even on the front steps and right up to the front door. The kiddos asked, "Daddy, is someone or something dead there?" I answered that I didn't think so but in my mind I thought if the enemy had his way there would be buzzards gathered at every house, on every corner and covering the whole earth. The enemy loves to kill, steal and destroy. Those are his goals for each and every one of us but God! God is a sustainer, protector, keeper and friend!

"FATHER GOD, FOR PROTECTING US FROM ALL THE BUZZARDS IN EACH of our lives we say thank you. Lord we know that even on our best days there are vultures that start circling when they sense we are wearing down, giving out and considering giving up. Lord, we know that you are there and continue to speak life into what the enemy of our souls had planned to be a dead situation. The fact that we are even alive and here means something kept us and we say it was Your keeping and

covering. It was You who kept the buzzards from pecking and pulling at our flesh.

Now today we come to present our requests for all the people around this world who are in need of a breakthrough. With all that you do we can't help but wonder how you keep it all in check while simultaneously having time to entertain our unworthy prayers. So by faith we claim your reply to our requests. Father for cancer, remove it. For addiction, break it. For broken homes and broken people, mend it. For failing health, revitalize it. For our children, we pray for protection and wisdom. For our homes and needs, please supply it. For our goals, desires and purposes please prosper it for your glory. We pray for life and more abundantly as you promised us in your Word. We claim all these things in the mighty name of Jesus, Amen."

Hold on Family, I drove back by that very same house a few days later just to see if the buzzards were still there and to my amazement they were completely gone. Hold On, keep pushing and praying because you ain't dead yet. Come forth, because today is a great day, for your breakthrough.

HoldOn 2 Overcome. H20

Knee Time

The picture really doesn't give the true perspective of the space. There were over 2000 square feet of flooring to be installed in a short period of time and needless to say there was a lot of time spent on bended knees to finish the job. So if we're going to be kneeling, we might as well be praying.

"FATHER GOD, WE WHO CAN STAND AND BEND AND REACH AND WALK say thank you this morning. We lift up those for healing who can not do these things. We pray for those born with physical challenges that keep them from kneeling. We pray for the amputees who can no longer bend their knees. We lift up the elderly who live with challenges in their bodies that keep them from getting down there and getting up again and how could we forget those that don't kneel, can't kneel, aren't permitted to kneel because praying to you Jehovah is against the law where they are and kneeling may mean they will put themselves in harms way. Lord please protect your people in the places where they are trying to block people from worshiping you.

Today Lord we pray especially for those who are on their knees digging people out of the rubble after the bomb landed. For all those working on their knees after the storm passed, the earthquake ended, the mudslide halted and the other types of calamities people are facing all over the world. Lord, just like you said it would be we are living in perilous times and we just can't help but notice the frequency and intensity of these things that keep us on our knees. Lord, if people can believe the fortune tellers and palm readers how can we not see the direct accuracy of your Word in the current events we see played out in our world today.

So we pray that even through the storms people will be saved. Lord, we know there are others bending their knees with us today and so we lift up those that are bending under the weight of worry and the burdens of bills. Somebody needs a financial breakthrough, a good job, a way to feed themselves and their families. Lord, we know there are some bending under the pressures of addictions, abuse, and the heartache the enemy causes with the lies, deceit, and broken promises. We pray especially for families that are under attack, trust that has been destroyed and for those in broken marriages and relationships. We also must lift our young people to you and ask you Father to please keep them on their knees and out of harm's way.

Jesus, we thank you for getting on your knees for us. Please help us to be ready for that great day when you will return and every knee shall bow. In the name of Jesus, Amen."

HOLD ON FAMILY, ANY TIME YOU FIND YOURSELF ON BENDED KNEES whether it be exercising, doing chores, looking for something, or scrubbing floors, remember that since you're down there take a moment to say a prayer. I challenge you to make a new habit that every time you bend a knee to tie a shoe or pick something up, take that quick moment to close your eyes and whisper a prayer. God will hear and answer. Every prayer is just another chance for that breakthrough.

HOLDON 2 OVERCOME. H2O

The Let Us Prayer

It was a school project with the kiddos to plant vegetable seeds and document the growth process. We chose lettuce seeds, prepared the little pots with dirt and set them on the deck to sprout. Every day we watched, watered and recorded our observed results but that project was last school year. We had even forgotten about the little pots and just left them there unattended on the deck for a whole winter. Then one day I just noticed a little green speck appearing in one of the pots and with each day, after a rain and then more sunshine little green leaves broke through that old soil. That lettuce continued to grow actually bigger, stronger and more vibrant than the original experiment that we had conducted a year ago. I just couldn't help but see the lesson that the comeback, the rebound, the renewal, the breakthrough...will be even better than the original. LET-US (pun intended) Pray.

"FATHER GOD, THANK YOU FOR EVEN THE SIMPLEST REMINDERS AND encouragement that you still hold the keys to life and death. Thank you for your Word which reminds us to never forget that even our dry bones can be filled with new life, vibrance and prosperity. We come today lifting those needing to rebuild after the storms of nature and the

storms of life. Father, we lift those battling diseases especially cancer, diabetes and heart disease. We present those held in bondage needing to be set free from addictions, habits and even the bars of prisons. There are people not speaking and lots of folks just talking way too much. There are people entertaining the voice of that serpent and allowing themselves to be influenced by the spirits of dissatisfaction, materialism, adultery and divorce. Lord, we pray your Spirit moves in your family the church with the power to convict hearts and save souls. There are so many situations that we are facing that seem dormant and lifeless but please let us not forget that there is still hope.

Father, we bind and rebuke the attacks of the enemy on our families and pray for the protection and keeping of our children. Many are homeless today while many are inside but empty. Father be with the lonely. Somebody needs to go to school and another needs to finish school. Lord, I know somebody needs the right job and a way to pay these bills. Somebody is praying for their soul-mate. Somebody needs direction and there are important decisions to be made. For the people who thought things were going well and then things fell apart please encourage them. In the homes where joy used to reside we ask that you restore the peace. Whatever the case, Lord let us never stop praying or give up on your promises to hear and answer us. Today, because we have prayed it, let us see You, feel You, and let us be saved by You. In the mighty name of Jesus. Amen."

HOLD ON FAMILY, WE WILL PRAY AND HOLD ON TILL THE WALLS fall down. Those seeds were *not* dead, nor forgotten. They were just waiting for the appointed time and conditions. The sun would shine again to warm them and the rain would fall again to revive them, then the life in them came forth. That lettuce did it and so will You. Today, is a great day, for the leaves to break through the soil of your test to reveal your testimony.

JUST HOLDON 2 OVERCOME.

Divine Chain Reaction Prayer

The imagery ran through my mind and then the words fell off of my lips, "I need a divine chain reaction." Have you ever seen one of those long and intricate displays with thousands of dominoes that people spend days bending over to set up? There are international competitions and even a TV show airing about falling dominos. All that time and effort to arrange them then somebody pushes the first one over and we watch them all fall down. The rhythmic tap tap tap as one domino strikes the next one. The anticipation and tension while wondering if the chain will be broken at the turns, the steps or if maybe the match won't light. Admittedly there is a strange attraction and irresistible fascination with chain reactions.

In a simpler form there is the sport of bowling where people try to skillfully roll the ball down the lane to hit that first pin just right to cause a desired chain reaction. The first pin is sent into another and then another in an effort to obtain that elusive strike. In the game of pool it's when that perfect cue shot sends all the other balls scattering and bouncing into their respective pockets. Wouldn't it be great to start something and then just have everything else fall into place? Well, we can ask.

. . .

"Father God, can we come before you? Can we approach your throne? We bow our heads believing you are omniscient, omnipotent and see the beginning from the end. We give you thanks for ordering our lives even when we just can't see it. Father, we are going to say thank you even for the storms, winds and rain in our lives and then ask You to help us to see the reasons for them. We do understand that we are literally living on a cosmic domino display and you are arranging all our pieces so they will fall into place. We are pins set up at the end of the alley and balls on the pool table ready for you to send the right break. Lord, we have seen that there are purposes for all the trials, tribulations, twists and turns. Lord, we know what you are capable of. We have read your Word and know what you've done for others. We see some prosper and others at least have some joy and peace. Father, we are witnesses to prayers being answered and we kneel here today with nothing left but faith that all things will work together for our good.

We've held on Lord, each and every day hoping and praying that today would be the day that the same finger that etched the tablets on Sinai...that same finger that wrote on Belshazzar's wall...that same finger that wrote in the sand would reach down from heaven and nudge over that first domino of breakthrough and cause a divine chain reaction for us and in our lives. We need you today to set off all that you set up. I believe that there is no-thing that you cannot do!

So let faith activate hope and hope activate healing for all that ails your children gathered here at your throne because we believe you are our God and are working for our good. Lord, please finish what you started and we will give you all the praise, honor and glory because only you could do it. We claim a divine chain reaction today in Jesus's name, Amen."

Hold On Family, trust and believe. He is setting it all up and it will all fall in place precisely as He designed it if only we just hold on. We've come too far to let go now.

HoldOn 2 Overcome. H2O.

The Flood

There's a saying, "when it rains, it pours" but what happened this week will go down in history as going beyond just raining or pouring. Imagine a big swimming pool that was empty when it began to rain but is now filled with water above the 4 ft mark all due to rain falling for 5 straight days. Some estimates say 24 trillion gallons of water fell on Texas in December of 2017 and it didn't just happen in Texas but it poured rain in Nepal, India, Southern Asia and Sierra Leone in Africa. Thousands upon thousands of people are cold, wet, hungry and homeless after torrential rains that caused massive flooding. While adequate rain is necessary to sustain life on this earth, too much rain can be catastrophic. Some people pray for rain while others are praying for the rain to stop and our God is able to answer both prayers, at the same time.

"DEAR LORD, WE WILL GIVE THANKS EVEN IN THE MIDST OF THE floods. In the middle of it all there are lives that have been saved, disasters diverted and if for no other reason we are thankful that people are praying and praising today that may never have done so without experiencing a flood in their lives. We can't see all the reasons but we know there is still and always will be something to be thankful for. Now for anyone that lost a life or loved one in these floods we ask that you send your Spirit to comfort them and let the hope from heaven fall on them.

Holy Spirit please warm their hearts and remind them yet again that this is not the end.

Lord, we realize that these torrents of rain came from the clouds to cause death and destruction but you said in Matthew 24:30, 26:64, Mark 13:26, and Mark 14:62 that the day is coming when you Jesus will fulfill your promise and you will come from the clouds to bring life and restoration. So when we see clouds approaching we will not fear but instead remember your words and Hold On to the promises even more. Father, we pray that you just help somebody dealing with the floods of water, all the insurance claims, the cleanups and those dealing with the other kinds of floods. Those holding back the floods of tears and those struggling with floods of bills, depression, loneliness and negativity.

What we need Father and claim today is a flood of grace and mercy. Could you send a flood of resources, a flood of good news, a flood of healing and a flood peace? We know that a flood of love, forgiveness and hope are not impossible for you, Lord. You told us that you could and would "open for us the windows of heaven and pour out for us blessings that we wouldn't even have room to receive it" and that sure sounds like a flood so we ask that you let some drops fall even on me. We believe and claim a flood from heaven today because we ask for it in the name of Jesus, Amen."

Hold on family, let's flood heaven with our prayers and remember, after the rains, come the rainbows. Those are the promises we Hold On to.

HoldOn 2 Overcome. H2O

I Can Always Pray

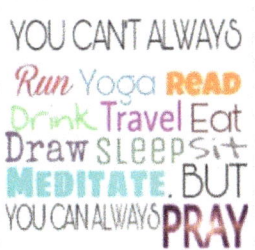

It was a light conversation about stress relief. Just a few people in passing were sharing their methodologies for relaxing and one woman stated, "I am a Christian, but I do drink." My response wasn't very loud because actually it was just an inside thought that came out of my mouth, "That's not a full-proof strategy, because you can't always find a drink but you can always pray!" It was just a thought but it was also the truth. No matter what, if we believe we are never powerless, never hopeless, never without options. Even if you woke up in the middle of a desert buried up to your neck in sand with nothing or no one within miles you still have options. Why? Because you can always pray.

"FATHER GOD, HERE WE ARE AGAIN WITH ANOTHER DAY AND THE opportunity to see the sun rise. Thank you for letting us be here as we pray for those families that have lost loved ones this week. Lord please comfort and keep them with your promises for the reunion in the New Jerusalem. Now Lord, we thank you for inviting us to talk with you. Lord please forgive us for putting everything else before you, for getting so busy that we don't have time for you and for filling our schedules with everything but quality time with you. We so often forget to put

you first and yet we call on you when we want stuff and when we need blessings. Admittedly we neglect to spend time with you yet we whine and cry about not feeling close to you. Lord, we can't help but bow our heads in shame if we even considered what life would be like if you treated us, gave to us, dispersed blessings to us in the same manner that we treated, gave, and blessed you. Lord, please have mercy on us. You give us the option and the method to openly commune with you at any time and we respond by being ungrateful and squandering the opportunities you give us. Yet you still keep us breathing, eating, sheltered and in our right minds because you still love us. Lord, we can hardly comprehend that kind of love.

So today our commitment is that we are going to do better. We are going to take these fancy phones and put You and prayer time with You on our calendars and on our schedules. We are going to make it our routine to talk with you first thing every morning and the last thing we do every night. We are going to give thanks at every meal, every time we leave one location and every time we arrive safely at our destination. We are going to ask you before every decision and thank you for every direction. That's our prayer today Lord and we ask you to please help remind us to always pray. We thank you again now for all you have done. In Jesus's name we claim it, Amen."

He hears and He answers. So make it a point to thank, ask, tell, consult, petition and praise your God in prayer then Hold On.

HoldOn 2 Overcome. H2O

The Hammer

Have you ever hammered a nail? I can remember marveling at my father's ability to drive even big nails all the way into the wood with just two blows from his hammer. He taught me to first hold the nail carefully with your fingers of one hand and then tap the nail head with the hammer in the other hand just hard enough to get the nail to stick into the wood and stand upright by itself. He would then quickly move the holding hand while at the same time raising that hammer in the other hand and bringing it down on the head of the nail hard with power and authority enough to force it all the way down into the wood.

I remember my first attempts and wanting so badly to drive those nails fast and hard like my father could and as you can imagine there were some misses, some bent nails, some nails struck at angles that sent them flying and some smashed fingers. It takes practice and today I challenge you to imagine that the wood is peace, your breakthrough is a nail and prayer is your hammer. Can you see where this is going?

"FATHER GOD, WE WILL ALWAYS, ALWAYS GIVE THANKS IF FOR NO other reason than we realize you have a choice as well and you don't

have to bless us. So thank you Lord for being here and giving us hope on this crazy earth. Now Father we're bringing it to you in bags, buckets and some by the truckload because we believe you can, you have and you will for us again. Father, we are determined to keep pounding on our situations by getting on our knees and by folding our hands claiming the promises of your words in Psalm 91:15, Isaiah 65:24, and Jeremiah 33:3. You promised that You will answer! It doesn't say exactly when so Father we will keep hammering on injustice, employment and for our families. We will keep hammering on our children, our friends, our church families and our communities. Hammering on our health, patience, forgiveness and love. We will keeping raising these prayers and hammering them down on Your promises Lord, until they go completely down and into peace. We ask today for strength, Father God, to keep hammering until we break through. We claim it, every answer to every prayer, for your glory. In the name of Jesus we pray, Amen."

Hold On Family, I hope you can visualize this one today. If you don't have a hammer right now maybe you can make a fist and pound it down a few times in an affirmation that you won't give up! You won't give in! Remember that Jesus allowed them to hammer nails through His body just for you and I and if He did that for us, surely He will provide the breakthrough.

HoldOn 2 Overcome. H2O.

The Sky is Falling

Yesterday a friend asked if anyone else's social media feed is beginning to look like Armageddon? She remarked that in recent days the disturbing things on her page had her looking out of her window for the four horsemen. I for one knows that she is not alone. Crime is everywhere with people being murdered on the streets and in their own homes. The spread of disease by even mosquitoes is threatening our human existence. There are locust swarms devouring crops all around the globe. Every day there are more commercials for more medications for more diseases. Epidemics, pandemics, wars and rumors of wars all around the world are claiming thousands of lives each day. People are unemployed, homeless and hungry while the politicians promise a better life for everyone. Who can even watch the news anymore? I'm here to tell you to Hold On because there is hope.

"Dear Lord, we thank you for literally keeping us alive and safe and we have to wonder how much longer before the sky really does fall? You did tell us in 1 Thessalonians 4:16 that there would be times like these. You said no man knows the hour but you gave us signs and wonders in your Word to look for and today even the atheist will admit that this can not go on much longer. Daniel and Revelation clearly tell

us what would happen but now Lord we have the internet and we actually see the accuracy of your predictions played out on these devices every morning, noon, and night. You warned us in Luke 17:26 that before you return our society will become like it was in the days of Noah but we never thought it would literally get this crazy. When we watch the news today we just have to wonder how bad can it really get?

So Lord we cannot with any intelligence ignore the signs or do anything else but believe that the sky is falling. We don't need scientists to keep reminding us that our resources of fresh water and clean air along with this whole earth literally cannot keep going the way it is right now. So if what you recorded for us in Your Word is proving true so far, then the rest must be true also and we are going to need you Father God to help and sustain us in these last days. Please protect us, put us with the right mates, deliver the babies and bless our children. Lord it's not beyond your power to provide the transportation, employ us, guide and direct us to where you want us to be. Even if the sky is falling we know you can heal our sicknesses, reduce these bills, calm and comfort the mourning and shield us from the attacks of the enemy who knows his time is short. Lord, we believe that the sky will fall because you said that one day You would come down from heaven with the trump of an angel and every knee shall bow and you will raise us up to meet you in the air. That's the good news we need to hear and focus on so we claim these and all your promises for you children. In the name of Jesus, Amen."

If you are reading this, take heart and be encouraged today that everything we see and hear is actually supporting and clarifying what God's word said would happen. So Hold on, keep pushing and praying. Even when the sky is falling, He is still on the throne so Hold On.

HoldOn 2 Overcome. H2O.

Data

Data is a very popular term nowadays. With all these new-fangled devices like phones, pads and watches, discussing data plans has become part of normal conversations. It's not uncommon for two people to be sitting, standing, even lying in bed next to each other but not speaking to each other but instead texting to each other. Beyond a doubt more messages are sent by email or text than are delivered to mailboxes. In a world gone electronic the more data you have the better and we can hardly survive without an internet connection. So I thought, DATA- "Does Anyone Talk Anymore?" People are typing more and talking less. Sending more and saying less. Messaging more and praying less? Is technology taking us in the right direction? If there is anyone that we really need to talk to, it's Jesus.

"DEAR LORD, THANK YOU FOR GETTING US UP THIS MORNING WITH A little something to eat, a few rags to put on and for taking our call without any wifi connections or data plans being necessary. I just have to believe that you are still God and you are still on the throne and so somehow whether I can see it or not you are working it all out for my good. So I want and need to talk to you Lord, directly. I am lifting the names, requests and concerns of everyone that asked that we pray for

them. I know there are people that are praying for a financial breakthrough and now since they have done their best they are relying on faith and your promises. There are some people seeing doctors, facing surgeries, getting test results, second opinions and they are worried about their futures on this earth because of some report or finding. Father, please heal them because somebody needs them. There is at least one of us in court today and others attending funerals who need peace and assurance. We pray for the families which include the children, the orphaned, the separated, the neglected and abused. Please don't forget the parents and grandparents as well. We lift those in need like the homeless, the lonely and the hungry. For our public servants Lord, the firemen, policemen, the soldiers and the ones who risk their lives for us to feel safe and those that are battling with life's inner struggles like food addictions and their weight. We don't want to leave anyone out so we ask you Father to bless everyone that needs a blessing because that is not too much for you to do. We claim the promises for each and every one of us. We pray today that you prosper us to be lenders not borrowers, the head and not the tail. We claim a change in our day, our lives and even the atmosphere because we pray and claim it in the name of Jesus, Amen."

There, we just called heaven, reached God and didn't use one single byte of data at all. Does anyone talk anymore? Yes, we do. We keep praying and Holding On.

HoldOn 2 Overcome. H2O

Who do I Believe

It happened again. I went into the store to get one thing and then my phone rings. While on that call another phone call comes in and so I put the first call on hold to answer the second call. Only a few seconds later and I hear the beeps that signal yet another call is attempting to get through and so I place the first two calls on hold while I attempt to answer the third call. All the while I'm trying to put my items on the belt and the checkout person is talking to me and I must have just reached the point of multitasking overload. I paid for my items, walked out of the store, arrived at my vehicle and placed what I had bought inside. I then got in the driver's seat, started the engine and drove away. I had only gone a short distance before realizing I don't have my wallet. AGAIN! I pulled over, called the store immediately and the nice person that answered the phone asked me which checkstand I had been at? I described the location and the young person that assisted me with my purchase and the person on the phone said she would be happy to go back to where I was and look for my lost wallet.

    I waited on the line hoping and praying while they went back to the very checkout station I had just used and searched for my wallet. After a few moments which seemed like days, the young lady came back to the phone only to report that my wallet was *not* found, turned in or left in any of the shopping carts in the store. Although I've prayed that "wallet prayer" way too many times in the past in desperation I had to just ask God again, "Lord, my wallet please." Then something told me to go back to the store. I rushed back through traffic to arrive at the store and promptly searched through every cart outside while battling paranoia and looking for suspicious people who may have nabbed the missing wallet I lost. Following the prompting of that voice in my head I went inside and back to the same checkout stand and... there it was, right where I had left it UNDER the credit card reader.

The question becomes who are you going to believe? Is it the voice on the phone, or the voice in your head/heart? I propose the more you talk to Him, the better you recognize His voice and believe.

"DEAR LORD, THANK YOU FOR GRACE AND MERCY, FOR FINDING *wallets and answering prayers even though we got ourselves into the same messes over and over again. How many of us are only alive today because of your angels, protection and receiving what we don't deserve while not receiving what we do deserve? Thank you again, again, and again and for that voice Lord, the one in our heads guiding us night and day. The one that says "go back." Lord please tune our ears to that voice and then teach us to obey. When man says no and things seem impossible. When there is no way out. When we are down to our last and it hasn't worked before and the car won't start. When we are already past the deadline and someone has betrayed us and it's all fallen apart. When doctors said no, there is nowhere else to turn and we can't depend on people. Lord, I chose to believe You and I claim your blessing. I thank you in advance and give you the praise in the name of Jesus, Amen."*

Whatever man says, I'll choose to listen and believe the voice of my God and Hold On. HoldOn 2 Overcome. H2O.

Acceptance

D o you *really* believe that God answers prayer? Are you willing to accept what happens no matter what happens? Do you believe that God knows what He is doing? Why ask Him then question Him? Which of us can see the future? Are you proposing that you know better than God by complaining about what happens just because you prayed for the answer you wanted? Isn't God's answer, *the* answer? Sometimes, along with asking for an answer, we have to ask for the wisdom and willingness to accept the answer that comes.

"DEAR GOD, WE COME OFFERING THANKS AGAIN FOR KEEPING US. FOR the angels watchful care, the food, the shelter and for the hope you give. We ask forgiveness Lord for our lack of faith, for doubting and complaining. Our request today is to erase doubt and write acceptance on our hearts and minds. Father we pray for a strengthening of our faith not only while we are praying but in accepting the outcomes after we have said Amen. Please guard our minds from even listening to the whispers of the enemy and his discouragements. Lord, we don't want to wander in the wilderness. We can skip the belly of the whale. Lord, please spare us the floods. We give you permission to bend our hearts and minds toward obedience, after we have gotten up off of our

knees. *Remind us to search your word for your promises and evidence that your ways are above our ways. Father, we pray for understanding, clarity and revelation in our lives today. Even if you have to make a donkey speak, please don't let us miss out on the blessings. Help our unbelief and grant us a victory over self to see, accept and follow Your will for our lives. In Jesus' name we claim it, Amen."*

Hold On Family, God doesn't make mistakes. The Creator of all is still creating our destinies. God said it. I believe it. That settles it. Now accept it and Hold On.

HOLDON 2 OVERCOME. H2O.

While We Sleep

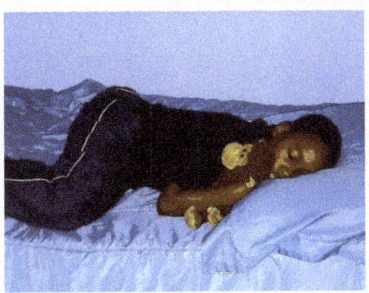

Have you ever experienced waking up in the middle of the night or early in the morning and just had a feeling that something isn't right? The first reaction may be to just roll over and try to get more comfortable but after tossing and turning you finally have to get up and go to the bathroom. You probably aren't thinking about it clearly at that moment but I propose there is more going on in the room than meets the senses. In these moments, the restless wee hours of the morning there very well could be and often is actually a battle being waged right above our heads. Maybe it's also happening inside our bodies, in the tiniest of cells as the enemy tries to attack from within. No need to fear, our God is there and always on duty, always protecting and keeping even when we aren't conscious or able to protect ourselves. He never sleeps nor slumbers, so that we can sleep and slumber. What a bodyguard, this Man Jesus.

"FATHER GOD, WE FIRST WANT TO THANK YOU FOR LIFE ITSELF realizing that we have to be alive to receive the breakthrough. Thank you for keeping us through the night and then waking us to continued protection every morning. Father, I believe that you send angels with

flaming swords to defend us from the attacks of the enemy while we sleep. I believe that you keep hearts beating, lungs expanding and kidneys filtering while we sleep even while we sleep. Lord, we know that some of us may go to sleep healthy, free from diseases and happy but wake up facing situations that are the exact opposite by morning. Some people wake up to separations and others will find out they are unemployed with only a few hours between shutting their eyes and opening them again.

So Father, since we know you're on duty and working on our behalf. Since we acknowledge and give you praise for keeping watch and working the night shift we ask that you also remember our special requests. In the morning would you provide a means of transportation and better housing for someone who needs it? Would you turn that no into a yes and lead that spouse to a change of heart and spirit? Would you arrange a job interview that turns into a job offer? Please send some food where there was none and remove the loneliness that has become downright unbearable. Lord, would you take away the aches and pains so that the need for the pills and substances will no longer be needed or desired? Would you please reach that child of mine? For all the requests that are whispered before closing our eyes will you please answer as you promised. Lord, we ask that you give us rest and a breakthrough by dawn and we will offer you all the praise and glory. In the name of Jesus we claim it, Amen."

Hold on family, read Job 33 and remember that even while we sleep He's answering. So rest well and Hold On.

HoldOn 2 Overcome. H2O

Midnight Shampoo

The kiddos had gone to walk Major the dog and as was often the case some animal caught his attention. It takes a strong attitude and a firm hand when dealing with these big strong-willed canines. Major took this opportunity to take advantage of his younger owners and broke away from them to give chase to some animal he had spotted. Now they are back home and relaying the story to me of how Major had disappeared behind a house. He finally reappeared from the darkness but he was soaking wet and stinky. Words could not justly describe the smell that invaded my nostrils as I stood there looking at this sopping black dog. To make sure he had not done some real damage that I would later be responsible for I had to go investigate just what he had gotten into. They took me back to the location of the chase and I went around behind this empty house and found there was a tall, wooden fence but the gate was broken and standing open. Inside the fence I found a long-since abandoned swimming pool that apparently had not been used or cleaned in forever and now it was serving as a sanctuary for frogs, algae, mold, mildew and all manner of organisms that turn water green and stinky. I smiled as I imagined Major running full speed ahead in hot pursuit of his victim as he sprinted through that gate and then discovered that there was a pool when the earth disappeared beneath his paws. I bet whatever he was chasing had a good laugh too when it realized Major didn't know about the sewage jacuzzi. It was a setup. We all walked back home discussing the strategy to sanitize Major. We decided to use an old, blue, kiddie pool in the backyard so we filled it with water from the garden hose and added a couple bottles of baby shampoo along with whatever else we had that smelled good. We wrestled him into the pool and gave Major the scrubbing of his life that night and he was grateful. We called it the midnight shampoo.

"'FATHER GOD, THANK YOU FOR KEEPING US ALL THOSE TIMES WE *were chasing things. Going where we shouldn't. Not following directions and falling into stinky places. We have to be honest and admit that most of these situations that we find ourselves in, we got ourselves in. We are a mess, sopping, stinky and we need You to clean us up. Sometimes we make the enemy's job easier with our strong-wills and hard heads. We leave ourselves open targets for his darts of destruction by ignoring the signs. We run with reckless abandon into the dark and surely find ourselves in the abandoned pools of life and you do it Lord, over and over again, beyond even our own understanding of grace or mercy. You rescue us and then shampoo us, again and again.*

Because of this history we have with you Father we have a better understanding of your love for us, enough to feel confident that we can still bring our messes and our requests to your throne. We come now to petition your assistance and we present our names, our pains, our needs and our shortfalls. We present our families and children to you for blessings Father. We ask that you Jesus take every one of our requests and scrub them clean until they are acceptable to you for consideration. Who else can we call on? Where else can we turn? If we believe there is only one true and living God then we must turn to you Lord. We need a midnight shampoo. We claim the blessings in the name of Jesus, Amen."

After that ordeal with the putrid pool was over and Major

was all cleaned up, he looked better, smelled better and had learned his lesson that fateful night. Can't you see Jesus filling the little blue pool with water, pouring in the grace and mercy, then stepping in with us to baptize all the filth away? The whole time He is smiling and lovingly scrubbing, tenderly washing our cares away. He takes us out, dries us off and then tells us to Hold On.

HoldOn 2 Overcome. H2O

The Healing Shadow

Some were healed or blessed because of the words that Jesus spoke. Others had their sight or hearing restored as the result of Jesus's touch and there were some that had tried everything and felt they had nothing to lose, for them it was their faith *in* Jesus that sent them searching for Him and brought them healing. There were however some as recorded in Acts 5:15 that were so sick, so weak, so hopeless and broken that they couldn't even walk and so they had to be carried by someone else who would then lay them in the path of the apostle Peter hoping that his passing shadow might inadvertently touch them and cause them to be healed. Sometimes, all we need is a little faith and the shadow.

"Thank you Father for all the things you've done to make it possible for us to even be alive and call on Your name. Thank you for eyes that see, brains that function, legs that can walk and fingers that can move to type messages that travel over the internet which we can't even see. I say thank you for the encouragements in your Word that speak life and hope into our tired situations. So today we come to claim a promise in the form of a touch. Lord, we are still here trying to stay close to you. Some of us have afflictions that are readily visible but there are others of us who may look good on the outside but are empty, lonely, depressed and too ashamed to ask for help.

Father, I pray you pass your shadow over our families to cover our children, marriages and all relationships. Father God please come near so that your shadow will fall on our hopes, dreams, plans and the ministries of those wanting to help others. Father, pass over those in pain, needing medical care, waiting on treatments and needing the money for medical procedures. We always ask for special blessings on those that are fighting the good fight against cancer. We are not claiming to be righteous but we have been faithful and we are your children calling on you Father for the healing of the nations. If it's nothing more than the shadow then we believe that is all it will take. We thank you and give you praise in advance for what you will do in the name of Jesus, Amen."

Hold on family, the Son always casts His shadow. Just wait for it and Hold On.

HoldOn 2 Overcome. H2O

Take Us Home

The famous golfer Tiger Woods isn't the first person to fall asleep behind the wheel while driving. I've done it more than once myself. The picture that accompanies this message depicts what occurred just days ago. The woman who owns the car in the picture relayed the story of how she had been suddenly awakened from sleep by the sound of scraping metal and an abrupt jolt. She reported that she opened her eyes and remembered the reason that she was in the driver's seat and holding the steering wheel is because she had been driving her car. Her car was lodged against the guardrail. She must have been so tired that she had fallen asleep at the wheel while driving. Have you ever tried to fight off sleep while driving? Have you ever experienced waking up in your car, at your home, but not remembering driving home or how in the world you even got there? Family, one thing I've experienced and I know for sure is that there are angels that protect and keep us and my guardian angel knows how to drive. As a matter of fact, angels often take us home.

"FATHER GOD, FOR ALL THE MILES OF SAFE-KEEPING, PROTECTING, shielding and blocking. For keeping us on the roads during the rain,

snow and winds. For keeping us in our lane and keeping them in theirs more times than we could ever count. We remember some near-death experiences and we shook our heads imagining all the ways things could have gone wrong. We shuddered as we thought of our family members and how their lives would be different without us. We know that we have stared death in the face on these roads and were snatched from the grasp of the enemy time and time again.

But it wasn't only in cars that you've kept us. You were there when we were walking and when we stepped on and off the airplanes. You kept the boats from sinking when we were onboard and the trains on the tracks when we were passengers. Every time we stepped onto a motorcycle or rode a scooter. Even when riding a bicycle we need your protection because it is dangerous and I can personally testify to how you kept me when I have fallen. Lord, we can't ride a skateboard without running the risk of killing ourselves and so we acknowledge that if you kept us, it surely was for a reason. We owe you Father for so much. What is it you want us to do for You Lord, today and tomorrow? We've seen the wonders and we know that you're not finished with us yet. There is more work to be done and so we ask that you please take us the rest of the way home.

You've protected, so now please provide. You've held us, so please now help us. You've restrained, please now restore. We know that within your arms neither disease nor addiction, poverty nor arrest, friend nor foe can derail the plans you have for us. So please fix some marriages and change some children's hearts. Reveal the job and the plan Lord. I pray in the mighty name of Jesus that someone who reads these words and makes them their petition will be blessed with all that they need to complete this leg of their journey and then we will give you the glory. On that great day when you return, please take us home to be with you forever. Amen."

Hold On. Hold On. Hold On. We aren't home yet, but with each mile and each moment we get closer. Keep praying, claiming and Hold On. HoldOn 2 Overcome. H2O.

Sustain Us

The Biblical book of Exodus records a journey. A large group of men, women and children of all ages along with their animals were all trekking through a wilderness being led by God to find a land of peace and fulfilled promises. It sounds like an epic journey. As it is written in chapter 16 they find themselves feeling weary after 10 weeks of walking and waiting, wondering and worrying. They complained that they would rather have stayed in Egypt as slaves and died there, at least they would have had their favorite foods to eat. The guiding cloud by day and the pillar of fire by night was not enough to encourage them. Walking through the middle of a sea on dry land wasn't enough to convince them. Seeing the entire Egyptian army vanish before their eyes wasn't enough to persuade them that God will sustain them.

With all the miracles we've seen, is our faith any stronger than theirs today? They saw the wonders, we've seen some wonders. They stepped out on faith. We've stepped out on faith. They sought freedom. We seek freedom. They suffered pain. We've suffered pain. They wanted a better life. We want a better life. They had families. We have families. They needed a miracle. We need a miracle. It was no turning back, life or death for them and if God doesn't sustain us it's life or death for us too. Today we need to know that He will sustain us on our journeys as well. We can start by asking Him.

"Lord, we thank you because we can testify that we have lived through some things and have seen some desert crossings. We have faced plagues and if not frogs or flies surely we have had to contend with darkness and blood. Just being honest Lord we too have been weary and felt defeated. When the celebrations and shouts of jubilation had ended and we were left to cross the hot, dry wasteland alone. We're trying not to complain but we just can't help but look back to the life we left behind to follow you Father and think about some of the things we called comforts. Although our situation was a mess, at least we had food. Even though we felt in our hearts that the relationship wasn't right, at least we had somebody. Even though we knew we shouldn't be doing it, at least we had some fun and joy. Although it was bad for us, it still tasted good. We had some money and could at least pay the bills. We had a place to call home and now Lord we are trying to follow your instruction so we have left behind our previous lives and now we need you to sustain us on the journey to the next. You know what we need and when. Lord please encourage us and give us strength. Please send angels like you said you would. Lord, you kept them, please keep us. You sent the manna to them and the Word says it was sweet. So we are expecting some modern-day manna to fall for us today and we promise to tell the world about how the one and only true and living God hears and answers our prayers, keeps His promises and sustains His children when they need Him most. For this we offer our praise, Amen."

No matter how comfortable we may become, this is not our home. We have been and always will be slaves here but our Father has prepared a place for us and he promised He would come back to get us and take us there to be with Him. So don't you even think about giving up while on your journey.

Hold On. HoldOn 2 Overcome. H2O

Out With The Old

Coming across an old picture of yourself is often amusing if not slightly confusing. If it's a really old picture you may have to try to remember that place, space and time that coincides with the outfit, maybe even the other people in the picture. Where are they now and what was I thinking wearing *that* with *them*? Honestly, was that outfit ever in style? Well they say hindsight is clearer and sometimes when looking back we realize that the past belongs and should remain, in the past. Sometimes it's best to just move forward. Out with the old.

"FATHER GOD, WE ACKNOWLEDGE THAT IT REALLY MUST HAVE BEEN you because it surely wasn't me nor my wisdom that has been the sustaining force so far. Father there must be things called grace and mercy because in my past I sho 'nuff made the wrong decisions, stupid choices, followed the wrong paths and got with all the wrong people. So I thank you for keeping me considering all the messes I've made in the past and removing the guilt so I don't have to hash over it or beat myself up with the memories of my mistakes.

Lord, I'm beginning to get it. Your ways are not our ways so what usually stains in our world washes in yours. Lord, I am asking for forgiveness for all the old thoughts and deeds.

Although I know I will have to live with some consequences of my past I come now as the repentant child asking forgiveness so I can claim the promises of hope for today and tomorrow.

Lord, we thank you and claim the new beginnings, new friends, new places and the new purpose according to Your calling because of You we have a new chance to get it right this time. Please heal the scars of our pasts and renew a right spirit within us. Lord, I pray out with the old and in with the new in Jesus' name, Amen."

Hold On Family once we've asked God to make changes. Be prepared for things to change. Don't be upset if your plans are altered suddenly or when people are removed from your life. Sometimes, it's just God saying out with the old and He never just leaves the space empty. He also fulfills so hold on.

HoldOn 2 Overcome. H2O.

The Inside

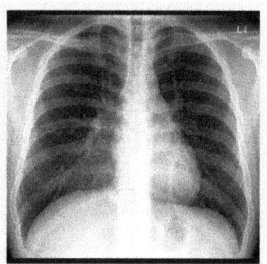

I have a friend that is a great automobile mechanic. I was in his vicinity and so I stopped by his shop for a quick hello. He looked rather serious and asked me to pray for his health. After a short conversation he excused himself and walked away, returning quickly with a big yellow envelope that he then opened. He proceeded to pull out films, scans and scopes revealing the insides of his body. He expertly points to certain areas of his anatomy and reports the concerns associated with the corresponding dots and blurs. The evidence presented here was beyond a shadow of a doubt serious and so we set the envelope and films to rest on a parked car as each of us placed one hand on them while joining our other free hands together and we prayed for what's on the inside.

"FATHER GOD WE COME NOW GIVING THANKS FOR THE LIFE, HEALTH and the strength we have been blessed with. We know that right now there are many that would trade places with us just to be able to get out of bed, to stand on their own, to see a face, to hear a song or to walk across a room. But Father there are a lot of us today facing attacks in mind, body and spirit and so we come now to claim a healing. We thank you for modern medical technology that helps to detect problems and for being able to see doctors and visit treatment facilities. We thank

you for insurance to help us pay the bills, for transportation to get to our appointments and for the hope of getting better.

Father, we come because we believe that you are our creator. We know that you never intended anything but abundant life and joy but now we are dealing with this sin thing and its repercussions that affects our minds and bodies. We have to be honest and ask forgiveness for the parts we have played in the destruction of our own bodies and health. Please help us to do better, make better choices and adopt lifestyles that will defend against diseases and death. Father, you said hope. You said life. You said blessings that we wouldn't have room to receive. Father there are cells that are out of order and we bind and rebuke the enemy of cancer and every other "itis", "noma", and "osis." And father for those of us with broken hearts, crushed spirits and addicted minds we pray for healing and not just back to our previous conditions that we were in but please make even better than we were before. Lord, we pray for healing for everyone. Come by here and turn the medical world upside down with what you will do for us your children. There will be no doubt that it was not by man's hands but by the One and Only True and Living healer that fixes people from the inside out! In that mighty name we pray and claim it done, Amen."

Now we have given it to our creator and healer. There is nothing more to do but keep going and keep holding. Because today, is a great day, for my miracle on the inside.

HoldOn 2 Overcome. H2O

Anytime, Anywhere

I answered the phone and the voice on the other end quickly asked if I could pray. I was taken a little by surprise and wasn't quite clear on the circumstances for the request and so I asked what did the caller mean? The caller repeated the question and asked if I was in a place where I could pray right now. My mind danced around the question and the whole concept of whether or not there is an appropriate time and place to pray? In that moment the answer came as a question that I posed to the caller, "Where and when could I ever be in a position that I could *not* pray? Yes, I can pray right here, right now, forever and always."

"FATHER GOD, THANK YOU FOR THIS ABILITY YOU GAVE US TO PRAY, to talk to you whenever, wherever, sitting, standing, even laying down when we don't have the strength to stand. Father, you made it so every one of us can practice telepathy and communicate with our minds because we can even think a prayer to you. We can pray for ourselves and we can pray for others. We can pray for our futures and pray to forgive our pasts. We can come as individuals and we can lift each other as a group. Father, you even made it so we can pray for someone who doesn't know they're being prayed for or exactly when but a shift

happens in the atmosphere of their life because grandma, a neighbor, a member, a stranger, somebody prayed for them.

And so we come now Lord, believing and trusting that because we call you Father, you will say ,"Well done my child." We need you to make a way and then show us the way. What more can we do Father but repeat your own words from your own Word? Father, you said that if we ask then you would hear and answer us and you didn't leave anything out or off limits. So today whatever is falling apart please put it back together and for whoever is falling down please lift them back up. Please bring to life our hopes, dreams, desires and especially our ministries because we want to serve you with all our hearts.

There is someone that needs to know and have that connection with you Lord, someone that wants to give their life. There are those that have been waiting but are unsure. Father, we are lifting it all, every single name and request that comes to our minds and we claim it already done. We expect something to happen, something to change across this whole planet because of these words we have spoken. We declare a change in the atmosphere because of our prayers. In Jesus' name, Amen."

Today is a great day for an answer, wherever you are.

HoldOn 2 Overcome. H2O

The Help Us Believe Prayer

Martha Munizzi "Renew Me."
https://www.youtube.com/watch?v=cB8xorl9rBU

It's usually uncomfortable to express it out loud but a lot of people think it, feel it, struggle with it. To just come out and say I don't believe in God can get varying reactions. Just because I pen these messages doesn't mean I have all the answers? You think all my prayers get answered? You think I don't have files of old unanswered petitions of my own? Think I have it all together and some powerful, infallible connection? Think all my questions have been answered and promises fulfilled? Think I'm sure? THINK AGAIN! I too need help to believe and if we're honest who doesn't?

"FATHER, THANK YOU FOR STILL LETTING US APPROACH EVEN WHEN we're shaking and unsure. I believe you created us and everything else that we see because the other options that man has offered for our existence just don't add up. I believe that your Word has spoken to me. I believe that people have prayed and have had prayers answered. I believe that there has to be more than this mess and all these crazy people trying to get more of the stuff that's destroying them. I believe that this world with all it's self-seeking, self-serving and confused

inhabitants can't and won't last much longer if they keep going like they are going now. I believe that what goes around comes around but there are just some things that don't make any sense at all no matter how I slice it. Even according to your Word some of this stuff today is totally UN-believable.

So today Father, I pray that you help us believe. There are those at this very moment that are asking, hoping, testing, rationalizing and searching for a truth to Hold On to. Lord, I know that at this very moment, someone, somewhere is just staring at a Bible. Somebody has really tried, but didn't get the answer they were looking for. Somebody just feels something is missing. Somebody has given their life to you but it isn't changing like they thought it would. Someone is getting dressed but not sure where they're going. Someone is in a state of desperation grasping for a last ditch effort to do or die. Someone is trying like Gideon to get the answer they so need so badly. Some folk are setting a time limit and pouring out their heart hoping there is a God that will hear and answer them. More than one person has tried every option and exhausted every resource. Lord, a lot of us have been used and abused, struggled and fought, recovered and slipped again while waiting for a clear answer from You. We have studied and served, loved and lost, passed and failed, begged and pleaded and still we aren't sure who and what we believe. So today Father God, we claim the promises of Isaiah, Jeremiah, Job, Psalms, and Proverbs which all specifically say, "If and when we call you, you WILL answer." Help us to believe. Father please, help us to believe. We claim our answer, in the name of Jesus, Amen."

Family, here is an encouraging truth. Sometimes we overthink it. We are looking for the heavens to open and the angels to sing and if that doesn't happen we can think we aren't getting it right. Consider this, Holding On is believing! That's all it takes. That's why we just keep doing it.

HOLD ON. HOLDON 2 OVERCOME. H2O

The Open the Windows Prayers

Either you believe or you don't believe when it comes to giving a faithful tithe and offering. The motto that stuck with me is ten percent because God is God and five percent because God is good but in reality giving to God isn't about money anyway. David reminds us in Psalms 24 when he wrote, "The earth is the Lord's and the fullness thereof; the world, and they that dwelleth therein" then he continues in Psalms 50:10 by stating "....the cattle on a thousand hills are His." Verse 12 gives the clear authoritative perspective when God dismisses human selfishness by saying "If I were hungry I wouldn't tell you for the world is mine and everything in it."

Consider how Genesis gives us the record of how God created everything including the plants that they raise today and then harvest to process the cotton and linen used to make a special fabric. They take that fabric and further process it to become the 10s and 20s we cherish so greatly. The technical term for our U.S. currency is Fiduciary Paper Currency and the reality is a $1000 bill in itself has no value. There are only three fourths a pound of cotton in each pound of dollar bills which is virtually worthless. Now go read Job 38-41 and then ask yourself why would my mighty Creator need my money when He can create anything, anytime, anywhere He chooses?

Maybe He doesn't want the money. Maybe it's really about

relationship. The verses read: "Bring the whole tithe into the storehouse, that there may be food in my house. Test me in this," says the Lord Almighty, "and see if I will not throw open the floodgates of heaven and pour out so much blessing that there will not be room enough to store it." That's Malachi 3:10. Well we just settled the fact that God does not need us to provide meat for His house. He is fully capable of taking care of that Himself. The second part is an invitation to prove Him, test Him, try Him. It's an invitation to enter a partnership with Him. The statement however is backwards because He says "prove that I *won't* bless you." God has already promised that He *will* bless you and in this text He is expressing just how 100% sure the outcome of trusting Him will be. He's saying it's guaranteed and if you don't think it is, prove it. He's saying I could be wrong and you could be right, so do an experiment. God can say that because He knows during the process of investigation you're going to experience something. You're going to experience… HIM. What other God offers the opportunity to disprove Him? Just let that sink in.

Furthermore, this test also gives us the opportunity to look back and see that He's already done it and kept His promise. Imagine if they would have paid your last paycheck in pennies. Could you carry it? The fact is ten dollars in pennies weighs about six pounds. So if you only have one hundred dollars in pennies you will have sixty pounds of pennies to carry. Five hundred dollars is three hundred pounds of pennies and for one thousand dollars in pennies you will need a wheel barrow for six hundred pounds of blessings and you couldn't carry it! You wouldn't have room enough to receive it.

"FATHER GOD, WE JUST HAVE TO GIVE THANKS NOW THAT WE REALIZE you have answered our prayers and kept your word to us. Even though we may not always be faithful to You, You are still and more than faithful to us. So Lord we thank you for the things with no price-tags

like life and health, sight and hearing and the ability to walk. Lord we lift up those that don't even have those things and we pray that someone in want receives because we ask you to bless them today. Now help us Lord to be more faithful as we step out and stand on your promises. Not for the return, but for the relationship. I claim a breakthrough for someone that's struggling with a decision they need to make to trust you. I pray that they give it to you and that you reveal yourself to them. In the name of Jesus, Amen."

It's my personal experience that you can't give God too much. He will always give it back. I am learning that the more I give away, the more that just keeps coming. Try it for yourself and experience the confidence of knowing you have stood on God's promises and you know you have a blessing coming because of it. Test God, by returning that portion to Him and just see what happens. Today, is a great day, for those windows of heaven to open.

WHILE WE HOLD ON. HOLDON 2 OVERCOME. H2O

The New Jerusalem Prayer

As we get older we hear more about funerals, attend more memorial services and most certainly think more about death. Eventually everyone considers their mortality and what will be their end. We buy life insurance and plan for when we might not be here. As I contemplate these questions I am literally standing at a funeral service. One of the longest threads I've seen recently on social media was about what happens after life ends. Will there be a bright light and a long hallway, or flames, screams and a big red devil? We are here one moment and then gone the next. Some lives are prolonged with advances in technology while others are gone in an instant with no warning at all. If we keep living we will probably have to face the day when we have more friends and family that are gone than still remain alive. Even our planet with the melting ice and bleached coral reefs, the polluted air and depleted ozone layer is signaling an end soon to come. The scientists are warning us that this earth's resources that we rely on so heavily are not limitless. Everything has an end. Aren't you glad that God has a plan with no end?

"DEAR LORD, WE ARE THANKFUL FOR THE GOOD TIMES WE HAVE shared on this earth with friends and family and today we know that there are people hurting because they are missing someone and life isn't

the same without them. Please send the Holy Spirit to comfort them and fill the space left by the loss of life. Please remind them that you said they are only resting and you are the alarm clock. Please help those that are mourning to remember the plan of salvation and it's great hope for us all. I'm praying the blessing of hope for this world today. Hope in your resurrection and your promises that you will come back to fix the pain and misery. We have had to endure the sicknesses and the tragedies, the surgeries and accidents, the worries and the sleepless nights.We also pray for those who have suffered through the funerals, the wakes, the memorials services and grave-side tears. Lord, we are still Holding On because of what You've told us about that city you are preparing for Your children and that day when you will return. You said there will be one day when a trumpet will sound and all those that went to sleep believing in You will arise. And then the ones that claimed the sacrifice of Jesus and have been waiting for Him will begin to rise into the air to meet those that were resurrected from the graves all over the world. That day when we all get to see the death of death. We are sure looking forward to that great reunion with all our friends and family in the New JerusalemIn. Until that day please help us to Hold On. In Jesus' name, Amen."

HOLD ON. STREETS OF GOLD AND WE NEVER GROW OLD. HOLD ON and I'll see you in the New Jerusalem. H2O

We are Your Children

We are in the 21st century and man has advanced to a new height of human existence. Look at our technology, medicine, transportation and exploration of space. With all that man has become and is capable of, do we even still need to pray? Many people believe we don't. Many people believe there is no God and man is left to his own abilities. Considering all man's accomplishments, why are there still so many problems, if not more. With all the achievements of modern science, why are people still suffering with the same kinds of drama that was plaguing man a thousand years ago: the ravages of wars, disease, storms, crime, food and water shortages? Why is there still so much misery? The fact as recorded in God's Word is that God often times uses these problems to get man's attention. It seems that when things are going well man gives himself the credit and forgets about God but when things aren't going so well man will remember God and ask Him for help. Tragedies humble us when we realize we cannot save ourselves. "When we are laying on our backs, we have to look up."

Yes, we live in perilous times but even when I am helpless I am never hopeless or powerless. It's the relationship with me that God wants. What won't a good parent do for his child that comes to them for help? What won't God do for me, His child, when I go to Him for help? He only wants me to ask Him, call on Him, choose Him. Whatever happens around me as God's child I have the ability to go to my Father and ask Him to change it! I don't have to wait until Christmas to sit on Santa's lap and ask for things. I have access to the boss, the President, the ruler, the Director, my daddy at any time because I am a child of the King.

"Father God, we come today really thankful that we have a source for answers and we have your Word. We are thankful that we've had somebody take the time to tell us about you. Father we thank you for your omnipotent plan you designed and then for following through on it even to the cross. Thank you for allowing us now to be adopted into your family and to be called Your children with all the rights, the privileges, and inheritance as children of the King. That's why we can come boldly now to petition and claim promises. While others may not know or still not be convinced. While some are concrete in their traditions and others brainwashed with errors, untruths and hate. While there are even some who just downright choose to reject the call of the Holy Spirit on their hearts and minds. We, Father God, right here right now cry Jesus! (Help us Holy Ghost). Jesus, we believe and we need you to present our lives to your Father. Please forgive and save us. Why? Because we are your children, called by your name and so we claim the promise of Exodus 22:23 that if we are afflicted and cry out to You, You will hear us. In the name of Jesus we pray, Amen. "

Hold on family, there is a difference between the others and us. We aren't like the rest. We are special, chosen and set apart. While they may be wondering, we know who we are and who we belong to. We are His! All it takes to join the family of hope is to ask Him and hold on.

HoldOn 2 Overcome.

Call the Bank

I was in the grocery store and had made it to the checkout where I scanned my card for payment but then there was a long pause. The cashier turns slowly towards me and avoiding eye contact she hands me a little slip of paper that isn't a receipt then tells me softly that I need to call my bank. My response. "NO WAY!" Was I hacked or was I a victim of identity theft? I called the bank and was informed that I had reached my Daily Transaction Limit. My response, "Say what?"

The caring customer service person on the other end of the phone explained that for my safety the bank had implemented a limit on the number of transactions that occurred every day and that included returns and even canceled sales attempts. So I can't make my purchase here at the store, I can't fill my empty gas tank and most importantly I can't even buy lunch for my empty, growling stomach? While I was pondering the seriousness of this situation I just thought I'm sure glad that God doesn't have a Daily Transaction Limit because if He did I'd be overdrawn by 8:00 am every day.

"FATHER GOD, I'M JUST THANKFUL TO BE SURVIVING THIS WEEK AND Lord I know I'm not the only one. Every day there are more crazy news

reports and the world is spiraling out of control. Father, I can't even remember half the stuff I need to pray about nor do I know how to present it to you to make any sense. So I ask you Jesus to clean up these utterances and organize my thoughts so that they will be acceptable and can be presented to your Father. Lord, you promised in your word that anyone and everyone can be members of your family. You said we should all come to you. We can claim all the rights and privileges due to the children of the King. He has no limits.

So here we are laying it all out before you, all the weight, cares, wants and messes. Lord, we have come to you for what it is we need because we have seen your storehouses, your accounts, your portfolios and we know you can never be overdrawn. You Lord are truly limitless. So please now complete this transaction for us your children. If we have to wait a little while please strengthen our faith. Bless us Father and those we love, care and are praying for. Release someone, heal someone and restore another because you can and we asked you to. We will give you all the praise and glory, Amen."

Well, if you didn't realize it, we just "called the bank" and the response was transaction approved! Now Hold On, because today is a great day, for that prayer to be answered and your Father has no limits.

JUST HOLDON 2 OVERCOME. H2O.

Separation

After creation everything existed in perfect harmony. God's instruction to Adam was simply eat of this tree and live forever. However, if you eat of this other tree you will die. Adam and Eve having no other reference for understanding death might have asked what this word could possibly mean to them while living in the bliss of Eden. Maybe God explained it to them by saying if you chose to touch the forbidden tree, you will be separated from me. No more personal strolls through the garden together. Instead there will be distance, a barrier between you and I. Things will not be as they were but how could they imagine a time without God, when there had never been a time without God?

So satan the deceiver planned to exploit the naivety of our first parents. In Genesis 2:18 God says "it is not good for man to be alone." In verse 22 Adam and Eve are presented to each other by God Himself and are together but in Genesis chapter 3 we find this serpent talking to Eve and she is alone. Adam and Eve are separated. Have you ever wondered how, when and why Eve was "away" from Adam to be tempted? How did they get separated so that Eve was at the center of the garden at the tree alone? The method of the enemy was separation and in a simplified form the whole strategy of Jesus coming to earth, his ministry and even to the execution of His plan on the cross at Calvary was to correct this problem of separation. The plan is to reconnect us with Him down here, so we can be reunited with Him up there. Well, today let's pray for that connection.

"JESUS, WE THANK YOU FIRST FOR CREATING US. FOR NOT GIVING UP on us and designing a plan to fix the mess we made and for making the sacrifice to come here, give your life in our place and return to heaven to petition on our behalf. Because of Jesus we have hope for a reunion on that great day and so we come to present to you some of the examples of separation that we are plagued with today and ask for your help. Father, please encourage and restore first those that have been separated from their health. Father God we ask that you defend against the attacks of the enemy on our bodies, minds and spirits. Please provide medical attention and the relief of pain for those that have been hurting and suffering. We pray that every "osis", "itis", and cancer that affects any of us will be healed completely and not allowed to return to our bodies. We even pray to have the medical bills taken care of in the name of Jesus.

Father God, we lift those that are separated from their ability to provide for themselves and their families. We ask that you connect them with the right job and link them with the right people so that they will be able to go beyond just making a living but will also be placed in situations and places where they can be witnesses about your power and goodness. Lord, we pray for relationships and for those not yet united with the one you will provide, Lord God hold them and let them feel your presence until the one you will present arrives. We pray especially for marriages and ask that you build a hedge of protection, love and respect around them so that they never know the pain of separation and Father, for those under the enemy's attack of divorce we pray for peace, unselfishness, forgiveness, understanding and love. Lord God, send love. Pour it out in and around our homes and hearts. Lord, we pray for mouths to be silenced and ears to be opened. Bring to mind the positive and good memories while erasing the regrets and mistakes. Lord please bind the broken and restore.

We also pray for the separation within families. For the parents looking for children and children needing parents. For those that are hurting from the separation of losing loved ones we pray for comfort and assurance that you will bring them together again. For those separated by distance due to jobs or travel, storms or calamities, lack of transportation or whatever Father we ask that you bridge the divides of space and bring them back together again. For those separated from shelter please cover them and provide a place of their own. For those separated from food please feed them even if you have to send the birds like you did for Elijah. For those that may think they are separated from hope please let them feel your presence by a phone call, a letter, or maybe someone to cross their path to erase doubts. Thank you for hearing our prayer and for all the answers. We pray that we no longer be separated but reunited with you, Amen."

Jesus came to defeat separation. Let's claim it today and hold on.

HoldOn 2 Overcome. H2O

A Change in the Atmosphere

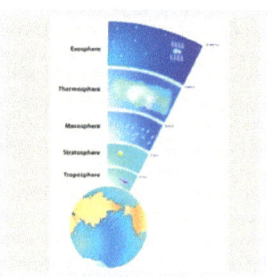

If you have lived on this earth for some time and enjoy being outdoors then you probably have noticed that our climate is changing. You can hardly watch the news or listen to current events without hearing phrases like global warming and greenhouse effects. Right now on the East coast it is February and it's the middle of winter yet yesterday there were record highs with temperatures in the 70's. Today, just twenty four hours later we have cold winds, ice and blizzard warnings. It's a fact that there is a change in the atmosphere. The supposed weather forecasters with all their satellites, scientific maps and meteorological studies are still bewildered and shaking their heads while they point to computer models in attempts to explain what they have never seen before. They sure don't sound very confident about the future but how could they with their recent track records? Man will try but he will never master controlling nor predicting nature and her elements. With all their technology they still can't beat looking up to the sky for their answers. Right now there is somebody out there, possibly you reading this message right now that needs a change in their atmosphere. Well we won't look to science or technology for what we need. For our hope and answers, let's look up to the heavens.

. . .

"Father God we thank you even for the constant subtle reminders that there are powers greater than ourselves and beyond our comprehension. Just waking us up this morning is not the only miracle we have to be thankful for. Science tells us that if the sun was an inch closer we'd all burn up in an instant and if the sun were an inch further away we would all freeze to death in a matter of moments and so we give praise and honor to you Jehovah for creating and ordering planets that hold their positions in space while others fly through space without bumping into each other. Lord, just looking up is both mind-blowing and awe-inspiring all at the same time because we know that if you can do that then our prayers are well within your power and potential. Lord, we claim the words of Mark 4:41 and call on him who gives commands and then the winds and the waves obey. We come because someone here besides myself needs a change, a shift, a warm front to bring a change in our situation. We are living and believing in faith that You are the master of the weather and our destinies.

Since it is only by faith that we can expect miracles we expect there to be changes in our families, our workplaces, our relationships and our minds. Father please don't let the atheist or the idol worshiper experience more peace or prosperity than we your children are able to enjoy. We believe Father God that you created it all and are in control of it all and so we pray it, we ask it, we declare in every situation that our God is mightier than anything we face. We will go forward today Lord believing that you are keeping us just where we need to be for our good and your glory. In the name of Jesus we give thanks for what you will do because we asked all these things in the name of Jesus, Amen."

Pray and Push On. You are not alone.

So claim a change and then HoldOn 2 Overcome. H2O.

The Referral

Who has ever given or needed to receive a recommendation? When you know someone that is so good at a certain job or craft that you can tell other people about them and suggest they use their services. When that person has an outstanding work ethic and skill set. When they do it well and have proven themselves reliable time and time again. When you have a relationship with someone that exemplifies mutual respect and true admiration. When you have the utmost confidence in being able to tell others about this person's abilities to solve problems and create solutions. That is just what I'm doing when I attempt to tell someone about the God I know and serve. For every situation, every problem, every dilemma I can recommend Jesus. I can make the referral but then you have to try Him for yourself.

"FATHER GOD, I OFFER THANKS AND PRAISE FOR ALL THE EXPERIENCES that led me to believe in you: all the keeping, protecting, healing and supplying. Last night I made another referral to you for someone that's sad and looking for answers and truth. Right now there are thousands upon thousands that need to know that there is a true, living and

loving God. There are needs that I know you can meet and so I've told others about you and given them your contact information so they can try you for themselves.

Lord sometimes I feel so helpless watching people suffer when I know they could get some relief if they would call on you and there are times when I am struggling myself and don't think anyone would want to hear about my God if I'm not an example of success and happiness. How do I represent You when I'm barely getting by myself? How can I be a spokesperson for faith if my prayers haven't been answered? Lord, why am I struggling If I am your child? Maybe it is why You had to come here as a baby and live as a poor man. So that you could honestly say you understand us in our weak moments, our temptations and all our tribulations and now I can look into the eyes of the homeless and say that I've been there. I can speak to single parents because I've been there. I can empathize with the betrayed, the slandered and mistreated because I know what it is like but the testimony is the fact that I held on and you did hear and answer and lift and restore. So if you are still keeping me, there is hope for everyone.

So I am going to refer everybody to you Jesus. Rich and poor, old and young, friends and strangers. I pray that you continue to bless me and give me strength to be a witness. I pray people see You, in me, enough to want You for themselves and then my living will not be in vain. I'm praying for my friends, family and the world today Father. In the name of Jesus I claim the breakthrough for myself and anyone that calls on you today, Amen."

We have the referral and we made the call. We just reached out to the specialist with all the expertise in all things incredible. Now we just Hold On for the phone to ring, the email to come, the letter in the mail, the doorbell to ring. He will show up, right on time. Today is a great day for that miracle.

HoldOn 2 Overcome. H2O

Out of Ashes

Here is the link and you can read/research it for yourself as it is going viral. Search for "Gatlinburg fire: Dollywood employee finds page from burned Bible."
https://bit.ly/3dkrn2W

I was awakened early this morning with my brother telling me this story about a burned Bible. The details seem rather impossible and incredible. Out of all the 3,000,000 individual letters of the alphabet that comprise the 783,000 words on the hundreds of pages that make up the Bible, this man finds this one mostly burned page in the middle of a massive forest fire. Out of a whole town ravaged by fire he finds a single page with just 8 legible verses on it that survived. Some may ask how is that possible and others may question the accuracy of the reported story? I say it was because someone was praying and they were praying for a sign!

"FATHER GOD, THANK YOU FOR LIFE AND BREATH THIS MORNING AS we lift those that really had to struggle just to get up out of bed and for those that had to struggle with not having any bed at all. Father, thank you for the internet and the media which you use to get messages to us that we need to hear at just the right times and for the miracle of this

story because you know I needed a sign today. Although the fire wasn't in my town and I didn't find that page you knew I needed to read about it. You saw me struggling here and you sent something to remind me and give me the strength to Hold On. I needed to know that the God I'm calling on, relying on, believing in and telling people about is beyond the realm of limitations or reason. You are the one God that can protect one page out of many in order for one person to see it and and tell one person about it so that one person can be encouraged to make it through one more day.

Lord, today I need you to treat me like that page. Please protect me, hold me, place me and then use me as a witness to your abilities and power. I know that just like those three Hebrew boys that were in a fire, you are here with me and so today I pray the promises of Isaiah 43 for myself and everyone reading this that when I walk through the fire I will not be burned and the flames will not set me ablaze. Instead, you will bring me out and make me a testimony to draw others. Nothing is impossible. All things work together and your word cannot return void. So I will Hold On Father God as You fulfill your promises. In the name of Jesus, Amen."

I invite you to read Exodus 14 and John 14. Over time and seeing the extraordinary ways that God works we learn to recognize His messages and methodologies. After a while we began to believe the impossible and expect the incredible. Jesus said, "For the glory of my Father, I will do it." That's a promise to Hold On today.

HOLDON 2 OVERCOME. H2O

G-man

This is the "G Man." Greg Kenney, as he is officially referred to. He is a vibrant, extra-intelligent and always-smiling high school student. While running a half marathon last September his heart stopped beating and just like that he went from running to fighting for his life. That fight has him temporarily and I repeat temporarily in this motorized chair. But don't feel too sorry for him just yet because G-man here is a life changer. I was walking down the hall at the school as he was motoring up. With another big smile he held up a hand for what I thought was going to be a hi-five but just as I raised my hand to meet his, he instead switched it up by spreading his arms wide and with a grin on his face asked me for a hug.

For a short moment my mind raced to numerous people, places and experiences. He wants to give me a hug, to help me, to encourage me, to brighten my day? Shouldn't it be the other way around? We embraced and I was forever changed as he smiled a smile of satisfaction knowing with that hug he had just added one more notch to his gun belt of contagious inspiration. The G Man, no matter what his circumstances, was on a mission to spread love. So today I declare to you and the world if the G

Man can Hold On, so can I and so can you. We all will overcome."

"FATHER GOD, THANK YOU FOR SPARING LIVES AND BRINGING BEAUTY *from ashes. I thank you for the life and ministry of this young man. I thank you for his spirit and willingness to help others. Today we come to claim the promises of your word in Matthew 15:30 where it tells us that they laid the physically challenged at your feet and you healed them. Father we know that you are still the healer, restorer and fixer and so we come as your children to ask that you heal Greg Kinney, and another and another. From this prayer let healing go forth to Greg and over all those in need of regaining what was lost in their bodies and minds. We pray that they WILL walk again and we will repeat Matthew 15:31 and glorify you God, the one and only true and living God that can hear and answer our prayers. In the mighty name of Jesus we claim complete restoration to our minds and bodies, Amen."*

You are not alone. Yes, there are challenges and struggles but God sends the "G-men" to remind us that if we just Hold On. Yes we can look forward to our new bodies and the streets of gold where we never grow old but there are also blessings and miracles for those who earnestly ask and believe down here on this earth right now. Today, is a great day, for a breakthrough. Believe, pray and hug. Hug On!

HOLDON 2 OVERCOME. H2O

The Life or Death

This week I had to pray literally for life. A close friend, a praying brother was in trouble and as time went on the situation grew more serious even unto death. It's one thing to pray about a wish or desire, a list of hopes or something for the future but if you've ever had to send up an emergency S.O.S to heaven to request immediate intervention to save the very life of someone you know or love then that's a different story and a different kind of prayer. If you think about it for a moment, aren't all of our prayers really about life and death?

"FATHER GOD, WE COME NOW SAYING THANK YOU FOR OUR LIVES today. Right now, at this very moment we know there are people mourning, hurting and preparing to say their last goodbyes to someone no longer with them on this earth. For those people we ask that your Holy Spirit comfort them as only it can. Show them what you have planned for that day when the trumpet sounds as you come through the clouds and the dead in Christ shall rise. Father, we now lift up more prayers for the people still battling for their lives. Right now there are people in ambulances, operation rooms, recovery programs, jail cells, doctors offices and courtrooms, all fighting for their lives. Father, we pray that life prevail in every one of these situations. Where death

prowls we ask for special protection. We lift those who serve in dangerous professions and risk their lives to protect us. For all those in uniforms, on battlefields and serving away from their family and homes. For those in police cruisers, on fire trucks, hovering in aircraft above forest fires and on ships out at sea we pray they fulfill their duties and return home safely. For those that drive over the miles of dangerous highways and those working to find cures for diseases, we pray that a hedge of protection will be around them.

For those trying to have children we pray for life to be conceived. For those exercising to improve their health and ward off disease we ask for vitality and longevity. For those who have been threatened with hurt, harm or danger we call on you to protect and keep them by dispatching angels with flaming swords to surround them. For those needing the basic necessities to sustain life like food and clean fresh water we implore you to provide in miraculous ways like you did for those in your Word. For the mentally ill and those weary from struggling with physical handicaps. For all the missing persons and especially the children. For those that will be diagnosed and those fighting disease and suffering through treatments. We pray for remission and declare no cancer return to afflict the lives of the survivors again. For the relationships dead and dying, the children hurting and the families affected, we declare life!

For those that feel they can't do it any more and the enemy has almost convinced them to let go we pray a shield against depression and suicide. Today we pray for life and as your Word proclaims life more abundantly. In the name of Jesus who gave His life, we pray life over us your children, Amen."

He is life. By His presence at His command death has no power to hold us. So Hold On, to Him.

HOLDON 2 OVERCOME. H2O.

The Order Us

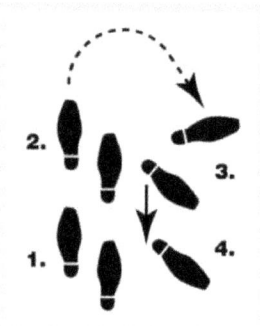

Not 1, not 2, but 3 things postponed the planned events of my morning and hence my whole day. With all the things I have to do, supposed to do and have on my schedule now this! Well let's hold on for a moment. Maybe that was God coordinating things like He has always been doing and like I asked Him to do. Remember that the Bible says that "all things work together for good" including the detours and changes in your schedule. If you've prayed about it, be assured that the future has been seen and every step of your life today is coordinated to bring the blessings to where you are right now.

"Father God, thank you for directing, redirecting, keeping and protecting. Even when we think we know the path to take we know that we need you to order our steps along the way. We know that what you say goes Father and so we come again to give thanks and claim promises. For the doors that shut we ask you to open windows and remind us to not worry. We can't help but recognize the craziness in this world and every day it gets even crazier so we come to you Father for stability. We need you to help us make sense of it all. We need you to direct our paths through the traffic jams, the detours, flat tires, and rearrangements we deal with day by day.

Father for the struggles, pain and sufferings that we encounter we ask that you relieve it if you see fit but if these inconveniences are what it takes to save us please be merciful and help us to bear it. We come today giving you permission to shape us and the course of our lives. Please reveal to us which way we should take and how long we should stay there after we arrive? Father God please send angels to surround us, our friend and families. Now let us go in confidence and rest in peace knowing that You see us and are holding us in Your mighty hands. In Jesus' name, Amen."

In Psalms 119:133 the writer David invites God to "Order my steps in Thy Word...." That's a request we can repeat today as we pray and decide not to complain about all the hiccups, diversions and schedule changes because God *orders* our steps.

So HoldOn 2 Overcome. H2O.

Incomplete

They are out there just floating around in space. The atmosphere is full of them I imagine. Incompleted prayers that is. Prayers that were started but never finished. Prayers that were imagined, but not prayed. People who were encountered but not lifted and that could be a shame because that means there are breakthroughs that have yet to be fulfilled. Storehouses in heaven full of boxes filled with unclaimed blessings. That is a shame. So we come today to finish what was started.

"FATHER GOD, WE COME THIS MORNING TO GIVE THANKS FOR another morning that we get to say thank you for answering our prayers. Thank you for allowing us to use our senses like eyesight and hearing. Thank you for allowing us to keep coming to your throne. Our special prayer today Father is for the incomplete prayers. The ones we've forgotten about or just gave up on just because it was taking so long. Father for the situations that didn't change and we decided we could live with it. For the things that we came to accept as being impossible. For the addictions that seem to have gotten the best of us. For the goals and dreams that we replaced with something we thought would be easier or quicker. For the prayers we were so sure about but gave up on. Father, what happened to the ministry that was going to help people and the invention that was going to change the world?

So today we would like to revisit some of those prayers. We ask again that you reach that young person that is living dangerously. We know that we still need to lose the weight, eat better, and exercise so we ask you for strength. We know that we are too easily distracted and often forget so we ask that you refocus us Lord. For the person that prayed for their sight to be restored. There is someone that is trying to make do but needs a better job and someone else that needs to take a vacation because they are always working. For the people that planned to go back to school. Somebody has been meaning to reach out to that old friend and someone else has vowed to leave a bad relationship. Please remind us that your word says all things and it is never too late to pray. It's never too late for a breakthrough. So today we ask for renewed hope and the determination to press on. We thank you again for hearing and answering our call, Amen.

Let's be determined to claim our blessings. Let's not leave any prayer incomplete. Never give up, never stop, never…quit…praying. Sometimes we have to encourage ourselves and a great way is by repeating the phrase over and over again that God is not finished with me yet. God is not finished with me yet. God is not finished with me yet. Our God leaves nothing incomplete. He is the author and the finisher of our faith.

So HoldOn 2 Overcome. H2O

The Truth

From children we are taught the importance of the truth but looking at the news one could conclude that most people aren't that interested in the truth anymore. It used to be that a man's word was his bond and we took for granted that when people spoke they were telling the truth. Today most people trust the media to investigate and then give them the truth. In the past we made decisions according to the truth and we thought, believed and expected our governing agencies to act on the grounds of the truth. We voted people into offices expecting the truth and the halls of justice operated on the principles of the truth but today that just isn't *true*.

FATHER WE KNOW THAT THE LIES AND SLANDER ARE JUST THE FALLOUT from the results of sin. As you told us in John 8:44 the devil is the father of all lies and so we know that people who are continually untruthful are under his control. You said in Your word that we can ask for anything and so today we are asking you for help and a breakthrough in the name of truth. You said all things will be revealed, brought out, made plain and uncovered. You said no man can hide from you, Lord. We know that no matter what people may say about us, you Father God are on the throne and in charge. Help us to see you, not them. You bring them up and you take them down, blessed be your name. Please help us to leave the vengeance up to you for the people that have been untrue to us and decided to include us in their untruths to others. Lord you said in your Word that you hate a lying tongue and you even added it in your commandments to all of us that we should not bear a false witness. For anyone who is suffering due to someone accusing them, misrepresenting them, telling a lie or withholding the truth we ask in the name of Jesus that Truth win this day and you lift the accused name out of shame. We stand on your Word as the ultimate truth and claim the promises in the name of Jesus, Amen."

Psalm 85:10 says that "Mercy and *truth* are met together; righteousness and peace have kissed each other." Hold On. Truth will win in the end.

JUST HOLDON 2 OVERCOME. H2O

More better

Have you ever gone shopping for something you wanted or needed and searched high and low for just the right thing? Maybe you were looking for the perfect gift and just when you thought you had found it and were triumphantly heading to the cashier you just happened to walk past another gift that may be better. You had the problem solved until you discovered something you think might be *better*. Just when you know the situation is under control and surely what you hold in your hand this time is the best option possible you get all the way to the checkout and have to reevaluate the previous decision because there is something possibly even *better*. Could there be something better still? Maybe I should keep shopping. The truth is as long as you keep looking there will always be something better. More Better.

"FATHER GOD COMING THIS MORNING TO SAY THANK YOU FOR BEING *the "More Better" God. Thank you for improvements, upgrades and all the accessories you add to our lives. Now Father we ask you to be our God, our guide, fortress and strength. Father show us and lead us in your will. Cleanse our hearts and minds in the midst of all today's turmoils and place our feet on the solid rock where nothing can be better. You see us and know what we need.*

We lift our own concerns but Lord so many are less fortunate than we are and so I ask that someone be healed today and be made better. Someone find a job today and work better. There's someone with a bottle, a pill, a needle that needs to get better. There are parents that need to do better by their children. Someone is trapped today, someone lonely, depressed and losing hope. There is someone battling a disease and fighting cancer. Lord, some relationship is under attack while someone else is praying for their children. There is someone being held against their will and someone running from your voice and so we pray that they will give in to your spirit and get, more better.

You said in your word that we could expect not just life but life more abundantly, which is better. So that is our prayer today in the name of Jesus. Not for our riches or selfishness but for your glory and honor and we promise to tell our testimony to the world. Please touch us today with your presence and that will make it all better. In Jesus' name, Amen."

Hold On, one day soon you and I are going to see the reason and purpose for all of this. All the things we thought were delays and unanswered prayers were really just the preparation for the "more better" that is surely coming. He promised us, so Hold On.

Just HoldOn 2 Overcome. H2O

The Others

The stories reported in newspapers and magazine print are usually broken down into categories. Some are on the front page with big headlines set in large print to grab your attention and mind. But there are other stories on the back pages or buried in unrelated sections. There was a child that went to school to report she couldn't wake her parents. The authorities responded and found both parents dead of an overdose and there was another child and a baby in the house alone. There are so many tragedies involving the weather in other countries that barely get mentioned at all. While some talk about upturns in the economy many others are unemployed, underemployed or have no hope of employment. People are starving, children are going missing, divorce rates are soaring. Lord, today we have to remember and pray for the others. Some things are just unimaginable. There are floods claiming lives in some places and people starving to death in others because there is no water for the crops. There are so many pandemics and atrocities in the name of religion. Lord, today we have to pray for all the *others*..

• • •

Father God, we thank you knowing we come into this world as babies with little choice regarding the fate we will meet. There are many people that did not ask to come here to suffer in pain or struggle to raise children alone. Surely no one would choose to be harmed by those that say they love them. What about the victims of scams that lost their life's savings and those that were kidnapped and held against their will? There are those that have been still going to work without getting paid but hoping this week will be the week they actually get a check because there is literally nothing left for the children to eat. Some are mourning but others are devastated because there have been multiple losses in such a short span of time and they can't take another funeral. How about those still unable to stop bolting to the phone on the first ring because they are still hoping and praying for the return of a missing person? Lord, there are people in places fighting oppression and fleeing persecution but with nowhere to run to. People listening to someone tell them they just aren't happy and don't love them anymore. There are people who don't have time or resources to take care of themselves because they spend everything that they have to take care of someone else that can't walk or doesn't remember how to.

Lord we lift these people, the ones that aren't on the cover but instead exist on the back pages. They are still pressing on because they are wired in a way that they just can't stop. There are struggles and strife but they press on anyway. We are asking that for every single person on the face of this earth needing encouragement today that you touch them, all of them, even the others. Lord, we are even willing to donate our blessing on their behalf if need be because we know if not for grace and mercy we could be numbered amongst "the others" ourselves. Forgive us and save us because you are our only hope, Amen.

HoldOn 2 Overcome. H2O

Should I

So many people got up this morning and started their day with expectations of happiness and joy yet spent the day unhappy and unsatisfied. Why is that? Maybe some are just on the wrong path. The question is how did they get there? Did they have a plan or are they just winging it? Better yet how many of us get up in the morning and ask God for directions? This morning did you consult the Father, the Creator, the one and only all-knowing and all-seeing God in heaven above? How do you know the answers if you never asked Him the questions? Did you ask Him about HIS plans for you today? Maybe that should be the first step.

"FATHER GOD, I COME OFFERING MY DEEPEST THANKS FOR GUIDING me and supplying all my needs. Now today I have decisions to make and I admit that I am not capable of making the best choices. I need you Jesus to guide me. I can not see into the future. I can not ordain or order anything with my words, thoughts or actions because if I could I wouldn't need you Jesus and I will never be foolish enough to even think that. I need you Father. I won't insult you with my self-elevation and then call out for you if sickness comes. I will not call myself a God nor offer anyone but you praise for my blessings.

No Father, I am the created. You are the creator and so I humbly ask that the purpose you have for me be revealed in my life. I don't want to make another mistake, wrong turn or misguided decision and so I pray that you open my eyes, block the negatives and lead me to the breakthrough. Where would you have me go and what would you have me do today? What words should I speak and when should I be silent? Should I go forward or wait? Should I press on or keep Holding. Will it last or could there be tragedy. Lord if the desires of my heart are not in line with your will I give you permission to change my heart as well. Should I Lord? Now please give me the patience I will need to wait for your answer. Please Hold me and mine while you work it all out. For myself and everyone reading this prayer I claim an answer because you said in John 14 that we could ask anything and that includes for your direction. In the mighty name of Jesus I claim the answers this day and forevermore, Amen."

Yes family, Hold on because He promised. He brought you to it. He will take you through it.

JUST HOLD ON. HOLDON 2 OVERCOME. H2O

Be Glad

It just wouldn't be honest to say that I always feel like praying. If you're human and Holding On, there will be days when you just can't pray. I mean really, how often do you see prayers answered? Well, consider the fact that maybe my prayers are being answered, I just don't realize it. Maybe I'm overlooking blessings and taking it for granted. See there are people that are praying and having prayers answered every day. So maybe, just maybe, it's the perspective of the "pray-er", the person doing the praying and not the prayer that is being offered.

Most of us are getting answers to prayers we didn't even pray. Yeah, it may sound corny sometimes but waking up this morning, free of pain, inside, with food, without bombs and not needing a wheelchair is a blessing! Can I get an Amen? Even though I may wake up to face new problems or another setback I'm going to thank God that it isn't cancer and if it is cancer I'm going to thank God for going with me on the journey and bringing me out on the other side a survivor. I'm going to decide to be grateful and to be glad. 1 Chronicles 16:31 says "Let the heavens be glad, and let the earth rejoice: and let men say among the nations, The LORD reigneth. Psalms 9:2 says I will be glad and rejoice in thee: I will sing praise to thy name, O thou most High. Psalms 31:7 says" I will be GLAD and rejoice in thy mercy: for thou hast considered my trouble; thou hast known my soul in adversities"; Psalms 32:11 tells us to "be glad in the Lord and rejoice, ye righteous: and shout for joy, all ye that are upright in heart." There it is. Being glad is a state of mind. Let's pray.

"Father God, I come today thanking you that I did wake up inside without major pain, without bombs overhead, with something to eat and not needing a wheelchair. Thank you for your Word which reminds me just how blessed I really am and for the hope you offer me. Instead of wallowing in my sorrows help me Lord to focus on all the blessings and be glad. Forgive me for my lack of faith and my short memory. Help me Father, to be glad and use me today Lord to help somebody, to uplift somebody, to remind somebody that they too should be glad and we together will give you all the praise and glory. In Jesus' name, Amen."

Today, the glass is half-full, the coin landed on heads and I choose to be glad. Hold On Family, we need to be glad. Give some praise and let's be thankful for all the things we have to be thankful for because today, is a great day, for another miracle.

HoldOn 2 Overcome. H2O

The Limitless

Ask yourself what am I praying for and why? Then ask yourself why am I not praying for *everything*? If heaven can do this, then heaven can do that. Do you find your prayer life to be monotonous? The same words the same way at the same time? "Thank you.. Lord bless…please help….amen." Are your conversations with people better, more in depth, even more interesting than your conversations with God? Why not talk to Him about *everything*: the stuff on the news, the people in your neighborhood, the rumors at the job. The Word says you can come to the Father for *anything*. Nothing beats a failure but a try, so why are we reducing our prayers to just some things rather than all things? Today, let's reach for the stars and pray limitless prayers.

"FATHER GOD WE COME TODAY SAYING THANK YOU FOR ANOTHER chance to say thank you. We thank you for the hundreds of prayers we prayed and the trillions of answers you've given. Now we come to expand our conversation with you Father. We come to ask for your intervention on everything we do. The things at the end of our prayer lists and the things we mention every once in a while. We know there is someone in our contact lists that we didn't think to pray for. There are people that we used to pray for but we have forgotten about over time. We have prayed for relationships, marriages, engagements and many times for our children but today Lord we want to ask blessings for those

that are hurting and healing while they are still in the relationships they prayed for.

Father, we ask for a clearer answer for those seeking direction. This week and even today show us what it is you want us to do to bring you glory. For all the little things that we intend to talk to you about but somehow slip our minds throughout the day. For the things that we just might think you're not interested in. Should we really pray for the small stuff causing big issues and the big things we gave up on too soon? For the promise we stopped claiming. For the old stuff that got pushed aside by the new stuff. Lord, you and only you know everything and so we pray today that you take all of it. Make the aren'ts ares and the won'ts wills then no one else can get the praise but you because nobody else even knew what was on our hearts. You can Father because you are limitless. That's the faith we stand on today. So we claim the answer, the revelation, the change and the breakthrough in the name of Jesus, Amen."

Hold on and pray for it all with no limits. Just like the words of the song says, "He Wants it All." Today, is a great day, for a limitless miracle.

HOLD ON. HOLDON 2 OVERCOME. H2O

The Matchmaker

T he story goes like this. A man boards an airplane in Argentina heading to Russia. Around the same time a woman boards an airplane in New York. She is headed to China on a business trip. Due to airline complications the man and woman both have unexpected layovers in Japan and find themselves sitting next to each other in the airport terminal while waiting for their respective connecting flights. They strike up a conversation and find they have a lot in common. They exchange contact information and within a year they are walking down the aisle to be married and yes to each other. Stranger things have happened and this one is true. Just imagine that at any given moment there are people right next to each other that are destined to be with each other. There are people on opposite ends of the earth that God in His great wisdom is arranging for them to be in the right place, at the right time, to meet their match. I propose to you today that God does not just match people up. No, God makes matches happen and not just with people but with any and everything. So today, we pray the matchmaker prayer.

"FATHER GOD WE COME AGAIN TO GIVE PRAISE AND THANKS. Considering we can do nothing we would be wise to thank you for everything. We recognize that only you are omnipotent but because we

are your children we can still ask you for anything. So today we ask you Father to be the matchmaker in our lives. There is someone that doesn't have enough and there is someone that has too much and we ask that today they meet because we asked you to be our matchmaker. Please bring need in contact with abundance. For those in the flood please send the rain over to those in the drought. For those who need help today please send someone who is out of work and needs a job.

Father, you know there are those praying for children and those putting children up for adoption. Someone has medicine and someone needs medicine. Before someone throws away food show them the person that is hungry. Lord there's a man praying for a wife and a woman praying to be a wife and vice versa. There are empty buildings and homeless people. Lord guide every one of us to our purpose today and let us be faithful to do what the Spirit leads us to do. Father your living word says that we can ask and it also promises us that you will answer. We claim the words of Psalm 85 which tells us that "mercy and truth have met together, righteousness and peace have kissed." In the mighty name of Jesus we ask today that you to be our matchmaker, our coordinator, our navigator and friend. Please put us on the path to intersect with the breakthrough you promised. For your praise and glory, Amen."

Hold on it's out there. Your mate, your job, your place. So don't be surprised. Today, is a great day, to meet the answer to your prayers.

HoldOn 2 Overcome. H2O.

Accelerate

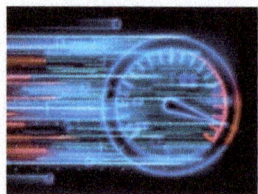

The word Accelerate can have a lot of meanings: to speed up, go more quickly, go faster, gain momentum, quicken, advance, promote, rise. On some days we need all of those to happen. On some days we need it, quick, fast and in a hurry. For those times there is the accelerate prayer.

FATHER GOD, WE APPROACH YOUR THRONE THIS MORNING TO GIVE thanks for every blessing and everything that you have initiated in our lives. We come in faith knowing and believing that you have and will keep your promises. By faith we claim the sovereign Word of Phillipians 1:6 that tells us that you are a faithful God and you will complete what you have begun in our lives. We come boldly and we ask that you accelerate the blessing we have been waiting for. Some of us have been praying and holding on knowing that there will surely be a breakthrough but today we want to ask you Lord to please speed up your answer.

Lord, we read in your Word that you are a negotiator. You allowed Abraham to discuss the details of the situation and if Abraham negotiated with you to reduce the number of people we are asking you to reduce the number of days until our prayer is answered. Father, if you can do it in 50 days would you do it in 20? If 20 is possible, could you do it in 10? Father, in the name of Jesus and for the praise we will raise could you do it today? Time is nothing for you God. You can arrange it, ordain it and speak it into existence right now. We have been faithful Lord and so we claim it because you told us our pleas cannot be ignored. You offered your help and we have accepted your outstretched hand. Lord please forgive us for our faults and we plead the blood for whatever may be standing between us and your plans for us. Please let today be a day we step further into our destiny. Thanking you again for all that you have done and praising you in advance for what you are about to do for us, Amen."

I know He heard us and now we just have to strap ourselves in for the takeoff. We've been patiently sitting on the runway with the engines running. Now there is nothing else to do but accelerate for the takeoff.

So Hold On, Hold On 2 Overcome.

Claim the Promise

It just came out of my mouth, "I'm not asking for, praying for, or making any more requests today. God knows that I need this miracle and I need it right now. If I am really going to believe that He is going to answer then I will start acting like it and just expect it to happen. I'll start looking for it. Even though I can not see it I'm going to claim the promise that it is done.

"FATHER GOD, EVERY UTTERANCE WILL ALWAYS BEGIN WITH THANK you. That much I am sure of. Then after I give thanks for my blessings I am going to start requesting blessings for those that need more blessings. Lord, somebody needs food today. There is someone praying for a way today. There are people walking and they don't know where they are going. Lord for parents who cannot supply the needs of their children and feel so helpless and hopeless. There are people struggling against voices and fighting urges they know are destructive. Lord for relationships, especially marriages good and bad. For paychecks to be corrected and issued on time. For the job offers to be received and the disagreements to be ended. For all the schools and places where our children go we claim protection from hurt, harm or danger. We pray for the staff members, the other students and their families. We declare this morning that the enemy has no power within the walls of any place our

children will attend and every attack from his demonic helpers will be repelled in the name of Jesus.

Now Father for all the people that are praying right now we just want you to fulfill your promise. That thing you said you were going to do, in the way you said you were going to do it, we claim it right now and may it come quickly. We declare that we believe what you have said and in the name of Jesus we claim it, Amen."

If you need a better understanding of what we are discussing here please read Solomon's prayer of dedication in 1 Kings 8 starting with verse 22.

KEEP PRAYING AND HOLD ON. HOLDON 2 OVERCOME. H2O

Brainstorm

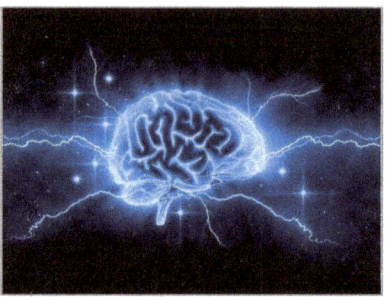

Prayer really doesn't need a plan, a formal format or a design. On a day like today with sooo much unbelievable craziness going on one can literally just let their imagination run wild and pray whatever comes to mind. That's a Brainstorm Prayer.

"FATHER GOD, I AM ALWAYS GIVING THANKS FOR THESE ARMS, THESE fingers, these eyes and my ability to connect with the people all over this world. Today I come without any prayer lists of my own. I just want to take the time to talk with you about the things on my heart and mind. I want to lift others and ask for miracles on their behalf. For that orphanage with children who never have enough, Father please send them food and the things they need. For people everywhere who are helping, volunteering and all the organizations that serve others, Lord please supply their needs today. For that elderly person that fell please provide healing. For that man or woman with the tooth pain, Lord guide them to a dentist to relieve the discomfort. For that person with the news of cancer please comfort, relieve and completely heal them. For those in the flood I pray the insurance will pay for their losses. Someone today is being held against their will, Father a miracle to free

them. There is a family looking for a loved one and I pray they are found healthy. For the young person hanging with the wrong crowd, block the plans of the enemy. For the couples under attack, Lord I pray that today they will experience unexplainable love and caring. There is a village without water that will receive water today. For the one that has to stand in court we ask a miracle in their favor. For the mothers who don't have uniforms for the children to go to school I pray that today they will receive the answer to their prayers. For those prepared to walk, a ride will come by. Father there are many that were sleeping outside but tonight they will have shelter.

Lord, I know you see everything but with so many things in the news I can pray for every story knowing it will cover somebody somewhere. There is Haiti, Ukraine, Louisiana, loan approvals, Korea, relocations, Alaska, relief from heat, Somalia, pain relief, Paris, job offers, Uganda, Mozambique, freedom from addiction, teachers, Turkey, India, school closings, Mississippi, Jamaica, Alzheimers, the safety of schools and college campuses, weight loss, bone disease, deadline extensions, the safety of public servants, finding mates, home purchases, the grieving, Pastors and church leaders, unfair hearings, engagements and weddings. It seems like a long list but it's really only the first few things from my brainstorm. We repeat the words of Psalms 143 to "Hear my prayer Oh Lord and give ear to my supplications, in Thy faithfulness answer me." For our good and your glory I claim it all in the name of Jesus, Amen."

That's what came to my mind, what comes to yours? Pray it, share it and Hold On because today, is a great day, for a long list of miracles.

HoldOn 2 Overcome. H2O.

Just a Sample

Have you ever been in a store, at a deli or bakery perhaps, maybe the perfume counter and then someone offered you a sample of a product? It was small but so sweet, so savory, so gooood that you had to have more. You actually purchased the product and have been using it ever since. A sample is a preview of what you could have, a pre-taste of what is to come. Well today, I'm asking God for a sample.

"FATHER GOD, COMING FIRST TO SAY THANK YOU FOR KEEPING ME and allowing me to talk with you again. I know this morning could have been different. I could be blind. I could be at the hospital. I could be heading to the morgue to identify somebody or in the morgue to be identified myself. Lord, I lift up anyone that may be facing those kinds of difficult situations today. I ask blessings for those that are hurting, mourning and in need of healing. I feel it in my spirit to pray for those that are struggling with attacks on their relationships today. I ask that you send protection on marriages, families and even those that are dating. It may not seem normal for a prayer but Lord I pray that you remove people that you see are not in our best interest and replace people that will hurt, harm or become a hinder in our future.

Father, I am coming to you because I believe you can make a differ-

ence. I believe you are the God that lives and changes things. So today, knowing all my issues, wants and needs I come to request just a sample of the blessings you have in store for me. Please Lord, just answer one of my questions or reveal a part of the solution to this problem I'm facing. Lord, I need some encouragement to keep going and a peek at the joy that is to come. I believe in your promise but is a glimpse of the reward too much to ask? You said I could ask for anything and so today I'm asking for a partial breakthrough until the whole breakthrough arrives. You gave John a vision that he recorded for us in Revelation 21 where he got a glimpse of the new heaven and new earth and so we ask for just a glimpse today as well. I claim it because I am your child and I am calling in faith for a sample of what is soon to come. Thank you for all that you have done and what you will do this day because of this prayer. In the mighty name of Jesus, Amen."

HOLD ON FAMILY AND KEEP PRAYING. SOMETHING IS GOING TO happen. No matter how small or insignificant it may seem you will recognize it as an answer to your prayer. It may not be some great miracle with fireworks and it probably won't solve all the problems but there's going to be a step in the right direction. Just enough to let you know He heard your prayer. The answer you are about to receive will only be a sample, so Hold On for the finale.

HOLDON 2 OVERCOME. H2O

For Them

Take a few minutes to watch this or search for the terms "Homeless in America." https://bit.ly/2SNMUrw

There are lots of people today right here in the good ole U.S. of A. that are hungry, going without necessities and yes even homeless. While we usually spend a good portion of our prayer time asking for things on our own personal wishlists, if we were to take a moment to think about it in the grand scheme of things most of us are already pretty rich or well off just because we have a safe place to call home, enough food to eat and the ability to change the temperature by pressing a button.

Today there are people facing some of the same problems that we are facing but with the added burden of not having a job, a bank account, a local Grocery store, transportation or even clean water to drink. The truth is any one of us at any time could lose our job or be diagnosed with a disease that could lead to poverty. Don't ever believe you are above or beyond the reach of a financial meltdown, a fire or the attacks of unscrupulous people. "If not for the grace of God, there go I." Let me tell you no one is beyond being homeless and I know because I have been there. Yes, for a long time I moved from hotel to hotel, slept in storage rooms and in my car. I will forever have sympathy and empathy for those that find themselves without a home and so today I lift those in prayer that are often overlooked and forgotten. Today, I'm praying for *them*.

"*FATHER GOD, I COME TO GIVE THANKS AND PRAISE FOR EVERY single blessing. I admit and acknowledge that I am blessed and highly favored. Although I may have my needs, requests and problems I want to ask you to do a miracle for someone else today. Today I'm praying for them. Father, I am asking you right now to send food to someone that needs it. If there is someone in need near me please place them in my path and show me what to do to bless them. I offer myself in service if you want to send me to help somebody that is praying for a breakthrough. Father, please open my eyes to those around me as I go throughout my day and bring the people to my attention that you want me to touch. I pray for enough blessings for myself that I will be able to share with them. Father please don't let me miss out on glory because I wasn't faithful in serving them. Give me enough but not so much that I forget who provides for me and answered my prayer when I was one of them.*

I claim the promises of Matthew 25 so that when you come you will be able to call me faithful and bid me to come to take my inheritance as a good and faithful servant. I claim the promise of your word that whatever I do for others you will credit it as done for you personally. Father, I pray that I may never have to go without the basics of life unless you see fit and know that the discomfort is going to help save me in the end. Please give me compassion and help me to show them that you care by my words and actions. Lord please bless them, keep them, restore them and save us all. In the name of Jesus I pray, Amen."

Hold on and help. That's what Jesus spent all His time doing. That is how we will Overcome. Give thanks, give praise, help and hold on.

HOLDON 2 OVERCOME H2O.

Right There

Where some people are well known at fancy restaurants or social clubs, I am a VIP at home improvement stores. I stopped by my local franchise and ran into a female employee I often talked with. There was a man standing next to her and she quickly called me over quite happily to introduce me to her husband of nearly 30 years. Interestingly enough they told the story of how they had both gotten dressed and left their house at different times that morning but were now standing here together having put on the exact same red shirt. Divine fashion coordination. Then she said to her husband, "Remember I told you that there was this guy that came into the store, that took my hand *right there* in the aisle and prayed for me? This is him."

I had forgotten about that "Right there prayer" but at that moment I was thankful to be remembered for something positive. In Matthew 25 God says "What you do for others, I'll consider it done for me." Family, don't you forget that any time you think you don't have anything to give, you can always just stop where you are and say a prayer to illuminate a person's life and give hope. When we do that Jesus considers it just like you stopped to pray for Him. Let's pray.

. . .

"FATHER GOD, WE THANK YOU FOR THE BLESSINGS OF LIFE, HEALTH and sight that allows us to recognize other people. Thank you for freedom and the ability to visit stores. For providing the abundance of supplies like food, water, clothing and even building products because there is someone praying for bricks or time to complete a shelter for their family. We say thank you. We come today willing to accept the call to give, to help, to listen and to lift those around us knowing that the blessings we bestow on others you return to us tenfold. Lord help us and remind us that if someone is in need we should share, right there. If we want a friend, be a friend, right there. Father please remind us to be bold and to take each and every opportunity to proclaim your goodness by at least praying with people, right there. Father, we offer ourselves today for your service. Then Father, we can claim the word of Matt 25:34 that cannot return void and says you will call us blessed and give us an inheritance. In Jesus' name we claim these blessings today, Amen."

Hold on Family, there is somebody out there needing and waiting for us to cross their path today and make a difference in their lives, right there. Let's keep lifting others and God will keep keeping us. If nothing else, give someone a prayer and know somewhere somebody is praying for you.

HE PROMISED, SO HOLD ON. HOLDON 2 OVERCOME. H2O

Better

I was listening to a new song that was repeating the old message that things are going to get better. Of course the concepts of things getting better, making improvements, progress and advancements are all a part of our human nature. Today there are whole industries dedicated to home improvement, health improvement and self-improvement. Literally from birth to school and then during our entire lives we are programmed to do better. But the question for the believer today is what is your ultimate goal? Do you want to fix this old car or get a new car? Would you like to patch the leaky roof or move to a new house? Do you love it here on this earth so much that you want to stay here or do you want Jesus to come through those clouds to take you away to something far better. For insight Read Luke 17:20-30 and 21:7-28. Let's pray.

"*FATHER GOD, THANK YOU FOR KEEPING US IN SUCH PERILOUS, selfish and violent times. As we look to your Word realizing that it was written thousands of years ago we have to wonder how it could have been so accurate? Lord, for those that are troubled by current events and are worrying about what's going on I pray your Spirit reveal to them your plan and your peace. For those struggling in so many ways please help them, heal them, restore them and comfort them through whatever is going on around them because you Father God have it all in control. Remind us to trust you. We claim the promise of Luke 21:18,19 that not a hair of our heads will perish and if we stand firm believing that we will win. No matter what the circumstances, hold us and save us, our families and friends. Lord in these crazy times let us be a witness to others that there is something better. Let the light of the believers shine bringing hope to the hopeless and joy to the depressed. We rebuke the attack of the enemy on our families and relationships and pray that tomorrow will be a better day where love conquers all. Lord please help us all to act better, do better and in the name of Jesus be better than we were before, Amen."*

Hold On Family, the Word does not promise us that things here on this earth are sure to get better. It actually warns us that before Jesus returns the world and it's people will become even more selfish, destructive and cold-hearted. But the Lord did promise us that regardless of the challenges surrounding us, we will *be better* in the comfort of His arms. The bad now is a sign of the good to come. Things getting worse now only validates God's messages to us and therefore we can Hold On knowing that if this much was true then His return is true also. Storms, wars, brother against brother...and then Jesus will come. Hold On, don't worry. If the signs are accurate the outcome is sure.

HOLD ON. HOLDON 2 OVERCOME.

If I hadn't

After a full day of running all around, if I hadn't needed to make that quick stop at the autoparts store...and their computer system hadn't gone down so I couldn't make the purchase... and I wasn't still standing at the counter when the man came in asking for a jump to his dead battery... and if I wasn't willing to help... and I didn't have jumper cables in my vehicle then I wouldn't have followed him across the street to the parking lot where his car was parked with his family waiting in the heat. I wouldn't have been there at that exact moment as my blessing was walking out of the grocery store. He was literally right in front of me. Psalm 37:33 says "The steps of a good man are ordered by the Lord" and Psalm 119:133 says "Order my steps in thy word." Let's pray.

"FATHER GOD, COULD IT BE THAT YOU ARE REAL, OMNISCIENT, *omnipresent and still answering my prayers every step of the way? Thank you Father for the hope and the revelations just when I need it most. Thank you for those little reminders. Thank you for speaking to me in a way that I can be sure that it was you. Thank you for answering my prayers and erasing all doubt because nobody else knew what I needed or prayed for but you. I ask, I plead and I give permission to you Father God to keep on working it out for my good and your glory. Let today be another day that I get closer to the goal. Father, please forgive me and cover this doubting humanity with the faithful blood of Jesus. Give me strength today and lift me up to know your promises cannot return without action and that there is that breakthrough with my name on it. If, Father God, if you just help me hold on even when it looks like thing are out of order I know you will make sense of it all afterwhile. You and only you Lord can make sense of it all. Please go before me and make a way like only you can. Please direct all things to work together for my good. In the name of Jesus I pray that my mustard seed faith will move mountains. Amen."*

Hold on, [say your name]. Hold on. My steps are ordered and it's all for my good.

HoldOn 2 Overcome. H2O.

The Cruise Ship

There is this cute little story about a person adrift at sea in a life raft. A rowboat comes by and offers help but the person refuses and chooses to instead stay in the raft. Then a fishing boat comes by but the person still refuses their help. A larger boat, then another even larger boat passes by but the person in the raft chooses to stay rather than be rescued. Even a helicopter flies over and drops a rope but the person won't climb up to safety. All the rescuers are turned away. Sounds crazy doesn't it? But maybe, just maybe that person in that raft is a hold on believer and they are waiting because God told them to wait. Maybe God has sent a text message, a sermon, a dream that said to them, "look for a blue cruise ship, flying a red flag, sailing due East and the band will be playing the song "Just a prayer away." Sometimes no matter how unreasonable, strange, or downright crazy it seems to others around us or even to ourselves for that matter, we just have to *wait* for what God promised us and told us was to come because what He says will happen, *will* happen. If we can take it, we can make it. If God said there would be a blue cruise ship.... HOLD ON!

· · ·

"Father God, thank you for your promises. Thank you for the times you did answer and the specific signs you did give. Just like Gideon we come to lay out our fleece and ask you for specific direction on what we should do. We are stepping out on faith and claim the fulfillment of your Word. Today Father is a good day for you to answer just like you said you would and in the way you said it will happen. We are still here praying, believing, hoping and trusting. We are working but still waiting for the outcome you said was sure. Only you know our secret prayers and you know what you promised. So please Lord, send the blue cruise ship so we know that it was you, the true and living God that hears and answers our specific prayers in your own specific way and you will get all the praise and glory. In Jesus' name we pray, Amen."

Hold on to it, Hold on for it. My/Your/Our ship will come in, flying the flag, and playing our song.

WE WILL HOLDON 2 OVERCOME. H2O

Evidence

I walked over to see the couple's new baby, a beautiful, bouncing baby girl that we had all prayed for. I jokingly told the baby that she needed a baby brother and both parents simultaneously turned to me and blurted out "Hold on, wait a minute now. This is what happened the last time you started praying that we would have a baby." I was literally touching an answer to my prayers manifested in the life of this little human.

Then yesterday while driving the kiddos home after school I saw a neighbor outside working in his yard so I greeted him warmly. We originally met a while ago and he had mentioned that he wanted to stop smoking so to offer support I stopped right then and there in his front yard and prayed for God's intervention to free this man from the grasp of cigarettes. Now he was so happy to report that the prayers and his efforts had proven successful and he had stopped smoking cigarettes. Then he said, "Tell the kids their prayers are still working." I stood there shaking his hand again, literally touching the answer to prayers manifested in this man's freedom from the addiction of smoking. There are prayer requests then praise reports. It is good to believe that God answers prayers. It's even better to touch the evidence.

"Father, thank you for your Word. Thank you for your promises. Thank you for loving us and not giving up on us. Thank you for answering our prayers. Because we know that you can we are asking again that you would bless the families and the babies to be born. We would like to especially ask blessings for those that came into this world with challenges. We know that you can fix problems, mend hearts and heal whatever ails us so we ask you to please perform miracles for our new beginnings today Father. We ask that you bless the new babies and new businesses. Please guide in the new relationships and new marriages. We ask for your presence in the new homes and new workplaces. We pray the words of Philipians 1:6 that you will bless the new things and finish the work you have begun in us. We need you Father from the prayer request until the time we will give the praise report. Lord, we know that nothing is impossible because you have allowed us to hear the testimonies of others and given us the opportunity to see the very answers to our previous prayers. Lord you told us that faith is the substance of things hoped for and the evidence of things not seen. When we couldn't see how it would turn out you allowed us to see that it did turn out in our favor. We have had victories. We have seen miracles. We have been restored. Thank you again for your miraculous touch that allows us to touch the answers to our prayers. Please go with us, live inside us and protect all around us. In the name of Jesus we pray, Amen."

Join us today in lifting your prayers. There will be an answer and it won't be long. I know it because I've personally touched the answers to my prayers. Today is a great day, to see the evidence.

SO HOLD ON, HOLDON 2 OVERCOME.

Just An Ounce

Kind of ironic isn't it the stance that our modern society has taken on prayer. They don't want prayer in schools, no prayer on the job, no prayer even in government buildings. Yet with every catastrophe in the news (which seems to be occurring literally every single day) the first thing they want to do is have a prayer vigil and the first people they call are the community's religious leaders. At the site of these tragedies people gather to lay flowers, light candles and bow their heads in what would appear to be reverence and of all things, to pray. Well today I will repeat an old saying, "An *ounce* of prevention is worth a *ton* of cure." The H2O version is if you stay praying, you don't have to start praying because every prayer is 10 tons of prevention. We don't have to wait for a reason or have an invitation. Mustard seed faith and an ounce of prayer, that's all it takes to move mountains.

"FATHER, WE ARE STILL HERE PRAYING. WHEN WE LOOK AT THE NEWS, when we talk to our friends, when we walk out the door to see the situations of this world today then return back home safely we have to say thank you Jesus for keeping us through each and every day. Lord, we come to you today to be proactive and preventative. We acknowledge

your power and ability to order all things including what happens to us. So we ask for protection, for healing, for supplying, for directing, for working, for restoring, for comforting and for SAVING. Not because we deserve it but because we believe it. You gave us promises Lord and we the believers will pray no matter what any person or law says.

You intentionally put the story of Daniel in your Word to teach us how important it is to talk to you on a regular basis. You documented the history lesson of how men made laws making it illegal to pray. You put it in print to remind us today that we may have to stand against oppression and be willing to die for our faith and our dedication to pray. Lord, you wanted us to know that if we were faithful you would be with us just like you were with Daniel. We want to be witnesses for you so please strengthen us, even to face the lion's den. Lord, like Daniel please bring us out of the pit unscathed to give the testimony of how our God performs miracles. We claim those promises for ourselves, our loved ones and this whole world. Help us to Hold On as we press on toward the mark of that higher calling. You said Lord that all things are possible and that You will answer us when we face adversity. So today we pray, expecting miracles. In the name of Jesus and for your glory, Amen."

Hold On Family, a half ounce of faith combined with a half ounce of prayer is a whole ounce of Miracles.

HOLD ON. HOLDON 2 OVERCOME. H2O

Not Goodbye

A while ago I started the practice of not saying goodbye. That word just sounds so... permanent. This week alone there will be three funerals for people that I know. Two lives were lost due to illness. These friends went to their rest surrounded by friends and family. The other death was a sudden accident and they never saw it coming. You just never know. So today we are going to pray for those mourning the loss of loved ones because we know that there are thousands at this moment in that situation. 1 Thessalonians 4:14, 15 says the exact same words, "those who have fallen asleep" and then verse 16 " the Lord himself will come down from heaven, with a loud command, with the voice of the archangel and with the trumpet call of God, and the dead in Christ will rise first." There it is straight from the Word. God declares that He *will*. Will is a definitive promise. For those who believe that the Word is God, that it is infallible and true, then there is hope for their future. We believers don't have to say goodbye. According to God's Word we literally can say see you later. The whole plan of salvation, restoration and eventually living in heaven with God rests on Jesus's sacrifice on the cross. He satisfied the requirement and then said, "See you later." For even more hope please pray and read John 14:1-6. Hold On and be comforted with the fact that Jesus Himself said, "I'm coming back to get those who are asleep." So it really is, see you later! Now according to 1Thessalonians 4:17 it's our job to get ready so we can go with them.

FATHER, YOU SAID YOU KNOW ALL OF OUR SORROWS BECAUSE YOU have experienced them. So you must know how hard it is to say goodbye to someone you love so much. Thank you for Your ingenious plan. Thank you for being willing to leave your heavenly kingdom and come down here to this wretched earth. Thank you for all the lessons that you left for us in that book and specifically Lord, thank you for taking all my wrongs and placing them on your back. For giving up your life to satisfy our debts. You did tell us that you were coming back so none of the problems and pains we are experiencing today will be permanent including our goodbyes and farewells. Until that day when you will return please Hold us Lord, comfort us Holy Spirit and please take away the pain of grief as we wait for that great day when we will be reunited with those we have missed so long. We long for the day when we get to see you and then there will be no more goodbyes. That day when there only be "see you laters" for all eternity. Lord help us to Hold On until the New Jerusalem, Amen."

Please share this good news with anyone grieving today. Hold On and be comforted because Jesus Himself said see you later and each day brings us closer.

JUST HOLDON 2 OVERCOME. H2O.

The Healing

I got another one of those have you heard calls yesterday. It was my third call about a life-threatening case of brain cancer in the last few weeks alone. Are we helpless, hopeless, at the mercy of this demon we call cancer? No! Can our God cure it, heal it, cast it out never to return again? Yes, He sure can. So what do we do? Pray! Any individual can pray the prayer of Jeremiah 17:14 "Heal me, O Lord, and I shall be healed; save me and I shall be saved: for thou art my Praise." There is also the "collective/plural" prayer of James 5:16 that says "Confess your faults (concerns/needs/ailments) one to another, that ye may be healed. The effectual fervent prayer of the righteous man availeth much." So while the individual person is praying their friends and family are also praying and now with this technology that bounces words off satellites in the sky to link us around the world in mere split seconds we can all come together and pray. Not just two or three, but two or three thousand, even millions of people can pray together. Are we saying that every prayer is answered the way we want it to be? Not necessarily but we are recognizing that we are not helpless to just sit and accept bad news.

. . .

"*Father God, we come to your throne now with praise and thanksgiving for You being there, accessible, able and ready to work miracles on our behalf. We come now needing and claiming miracles on behalf of those battling cancer and even more specifically brain cancer. Please Father, if we can ask anything then we ask that you cure someone in a battle with cancer. Father, order those cells to fall in line. We pray that you bind and rebuke the attack of the enemy on these people and their families. There are children that need their parents and parents that need their children. Just like in the Bible we know that you can cast out evil spirits and cause the demons of disease to flee. Please make the surgery, the transplant or the amputation unnecessary. We pray for relief from pain and discomfort. We are claiming complete restoration so the world will know that you are the only one and true God that is a greater doctor. You do answer prayers and heal when men thought it was impossible. Please guide and assist the medical professionals but it is You who will get the honor and glory because of the miracle they can't explain. We will tell it and they will show it. In the name of Jesus we plead the blood for healing, Amen.*"

Hold On and let's never give up on praying. There have been too many testimonies to accept defeat. He is able and today is a great day for a miraculous healing.

HoldOn 2 Overcome Cancer.

Still Here

A line from one of my favorite poems Invictus by Ernest Henley says, "In the fell clutch of circumstance I have not winced nor cried aloud. Under the bludgeoning of chance, my head is bloody, but unbowed." It is a poem about not giving up. There are a lot of poems, songs, even movies about not giving up but nothing beats a prayer. So today we will pray the still here prayer. It goes like this.

"Thank you for waking us and taking us as we come again to your throne. We are still here Father, waiting for your answer. Still here Father, trying to praise. Still here Father, working as best we can. Still here Father, serving. Still here Father, reading. Still here Father, fasting and praying in the mighty name of Jesus. As long as you are still there we will still be here. So we claim the blessing and answer to our prayers that will be revealed this day, Amen."

Now we give notice. "Did you hear that enemy? Be advised that I am still here and calling you a liar. Still here waiting because Jesus said. Still here praising because it brings victory. Still here working because He said that there will be a reward for my labor. Still here fasting because it helps develop patience and self control. Still here serving because what I do for others He counts it as done to Him. Still here reading because His word informs, comforts and heals. Still here claiming because I am His child and He promised me. Still here praying because I know what he can do and I believe it! Insomnia, debt, slander, addiction, unfulfilled dreams and all the rest. We declare right now that you are defeated because we are still here Holding On."

We claim the words of James 5 for each one of you reading this right now.

BE BLESSED AND HOLD ON. HOLD ON, 2 OVERCOME. H2O.

Never Stop Asking

Every day and I mean every day for the past few days I have been told about another tragic attack on someone's health. The "C" word keeps coming up. People are facing pain, debilitating treatments, surgeries and predictions on life expectancy. Talking to someone about sicknesses can be a very uncomfortable situation and we usually feel so helpless. Most of the time all we can do is say that we will pray for them.

I read a story about a man that had been blind for 31 years. Blinded as a child he had lived with this condition until 3 decades later the technology had advanced to not only diagnose his problem but to also restore his sight. So with the success of a new procedure he was able to see his wife and children for the first time. Glory to God. While he was living with it, God was fixing it!

That story was an amazing example of what it means to never stop praying. The impossible can become possible. Do I accept defeat, the diagnosis, the prognosis? Do I surrender and just get used to the problem? Do I give in or do I keep on Holding On for that miracle? To answer the previous questions the answer is no. Read John 9:8. A man there sat and begged for years before Jesus came, put mud in his eyes and he could finally see. I will not give up or stop asking. I declare today that Jesus is still in the miracle working business. I don't have to accept any situation. For every situation that seems impossible Jesus is the answer. Pray and ask for healing for his glory. We bind and rebuke you cancer for his glory. This prayer is for the person that is fighting against cancer.

"Thank you Father, for victory. I know cancer has always been there and you saw it. I know you saw my specific situation ahead of time. I know you allowed this affliction for a purpose. I know you will not leave me alone while I'm going through it. I know you are capable of healing any and every thing. I know you do not enjoy seeing me suffer. I know you want to comfort me and heal me so that is exactly what I'm asking you to do. Please restore me. Please take away the pain. Please give me strength and encourage me. Please console my friends and family. Please bless the medical workers and allow me to be a witness to them. Please provide the funds I need and the favorable actions of the insurance companies. I claim you as my God, savior and friend. For all you've done, for what you are doing and what you will do because I will never stop asking it in the name of Jesus, Amen.

Never stop. Never quit. Never give in or give up. Let your last breath be a prayer. H2O

Prayer requests can be sent to HoldOn2Overcome@gmail.com because we won't stop either.

Trust

❧

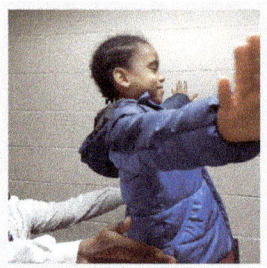

The story was told to me just like this. "You know I'm caring for my mom but I lost my job last year and have been struggling to keep a roof overhead. We were behind on the mortgage and facing foreclosure but I refused to put my mother in a nursing home. She deserves my love and care. She's in her 80s and has been diagnosed with Alzheimer's. The other day while her nurse aid was here at the house giving her a bath, mom just called out and said, "You know what.......TRUST!" A senior citizen supposedly with a diminished memory said trust.

"FATHER GOD, WE COME AGAIN WITH THANKS AND PRAISES FOR keeping us even when we aren't trusting. Yet you are still sustaining and providing and protecting. Father, we have to be honest because you know anyway. When things are going well we get distracted and forget to trust you, forget that we need You. We forget who is really in control then when the challenges come and the darkness of the enemy seems to cover us so completely we get discouraged and feel we can't even come to you for help. Sometimes we are so easily shaken and distracted but today we claim the promise of the Word found in Matthew 17 and Luke 17 that with just a little faith, mustard seed faith, we can and will move mountains. So we come to offer even our one percent knowing you can

provide the other ninety nine. Father, if you can do anything then help us to trust. Let us literally feel your presence. Give us signs and lead us in your will and your way. Help us to remember Lord so that if we have to write it on our hand, make it our screensaver, tape it to the steering wheel or just repeat your name all day long. If that is what it takes, then I will trust! Enemy, try all you want but I declare that I will be victorious because of that name Jesus, Amen."

Hold On and trust. Different words but one in the same, so are Jesus and victory.

HOLDON 2 OVERCOME.H2O

Til The End

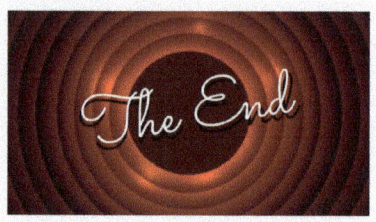

We were talking and my friend quoted, "The race is not given to the swift or the strong but to him that endureth to the end." (Ecclesiastes 9:11) I thought what end? Who's end? Our end? Wait a minute, God doesn't have an end. God *is* the end. Revelations 1:8, 21:6, 22:13 all repeat the fact that "I am the Alpha and Omega, the beginning and the *end*." So is it really too simplified to apply logic and say the race is not given to the swift or to the strong but to him that endureth to.... Jesus! If we just keep going and Hold On until.... Jesus. There He is, arms open wide saying Me. Lean on Me. Depend on Me. Hold On to Me. I'm the end to your searching, worries, ev-ry-thing, beginning and end.

"FATHER GOD, THANK YOU FOR YOUR WORD AND HOW SIMPLY IT CAN speak to me. I humbly come to you as the end all for whatever ails me. You Father God, who knows no bounds and can do all things. I bring you even my heart's secrets, my failures and shame. I admit my shortcomings and my need for your greatness and power. In the name of Jesus please answer my prayer and for all those needing an end today I pray a miracle from heaven because you promised and you said you are not a man that can lie. In the name of the one that has no end, Amen."

Hold On, all negativity ends with Him and one day soon the end of this earth will become the beginning of our eternity. I can't wait, how about you?

HoldOn 2 Overcome H2O.

Birdly Confidence

The scene played out right in front of me as if I was watching a great theatrical performance. First, a cat walked by. It was squatting low and moving slowly. This was a cat on the prowl prepared to pounce on it's next meal. Then right on cue a bird flew down and came to rest directly in the vicinity of the lurking cat. I thought to myself that bird better be careful. Doesn't it see the cat right there? Then I wondered why a bird would do such a seemingly not so smart thing with no fear at all? I thought about 1 Peter 5:8 and how it warns us that satan is like a lion seeking to devour us but then I remembered with a smile, "The bird really doesn't have to worry about the cat because the bird, can fly!"

"FATHER GOD, WE THANK YOU FOR THE REMINDERS EVEN IN NATURE that you are there. You go before us and protect all around us. You make a way for us and so we don't have to fear but we know there are lurking dangers and many feel like they've been caught by the cats of life. Big cats Lord, stalking our health, our finances, our families and our relationships. We know there is an enemy trying to trap us in anxiety, fear, addictions, pain, or whatever else he can come up with. So Father we

bring all our situations to you asking that you help us, give us confidence and teach us to fly. Lord strengthen us, lift us up and fulfill the promise of your word to raise our heads from shame. Lord, some are tired, some are weary and some are just through. Today Father God, we ask that you renew and encourage them. There can be no hopelessness in your presence so show them that you are there with them. Lord, in spite of the dangers and pitfalls we believe what you've told us and we are Holding On, ready to fly. Please accept our prayers and forgive us for all our sins. We ask it in the name of Jesus, Amen."

Hold on Family, 1 Peter 5:10 says "And the God of all grace, who called you to his eternal glory in Christ, after you have suffered a little while, will Himself restore you and make you strong, firm and steadfast." That's the promise to Hold On to today and remember even if you feel you can't fly, Jesus can.

JUST HOLD ON, AND FLY!!!!!! FLY ON 2 OVERCOME. F2O

The Children

For people who really want to feel the pulse of today's culture and get an idea of where our society is headed I often challenge them to go spend a few days in a local high school. So many people have ideals and opinions. Anybody can pontificate with their theories and talk about how it used to be when they were young or in school but to really get a sense of what contemporary norms are and where it is all headed take the challenge. Spend some time with today's young people to see if there is cause for concern. What about the next generation especially considering how many of these babies are having babies? Hold On Family, without a shadow of a doubt I know the enemy is waging an all out war on my/your/our children but we are not helpless or hopeless. If the enemy wants to get to my children, he will have to break through the protection of my prayers.

"FATHER GOD, WE COME TODAY TO SAY THANK YOU FOR ALL THE births and babies. We realize that you gave us the opportunity to better understand your love for us, your children, by allowing us to have children of our own. Children didn't ask to come here Lord and we realize that it must hurt you greatly to see these your babies, the innocent lives

and undeserving souls suffer. Lord, please heal a child. Let one walk and another talk. Allow one to speak and another to hear. Please relieve the pain of a child and return another child back home. Lord, please send some clothes and provide shelter. For the children that want to but can't go to school. For the young people that are incarcerated. Please give us the adults a discerning eye and a loving heart to want to reach out and help some children.

Lord, I pray that you bind and rebuke the attack on our young people especially in the form of drugs and alcohol. In the name of Jesus I ask for a repulsion rather than an attraction to the enemy's influences through music and the media. We ask you to protect the young impressionable minds and our teenagers that think they have the answers.

I thank you for your plan of restoration and the hope it gives us for the children. We ask that your presence and power be manifested in their lives and thank you for your plan to save each and every child when you come. You are a fair and just God and you made provisions for those who didn't have a choice or a chance and for those that have laid children to rest we pray for comfort and hope. In Jesus' name we claim an answer to every prayer for young people around the world, Amen."

Yes, our young people today are facing challenges never before seen on this scale but they are not hopeless and we are not helpless. Matthew 19:14, Mark 10:14 and Luke 18:16 all say "Suffer the little children to come unto me...." God *is* able, so don't give up on them. Tell and teach them to Hold On.

HOLDON 2 OVERCOME. H2O

The W.A.R.

Are you W.A.R.? Are you Willing, Able and Ready. **Willing** meaning you are asking for God's direction and have fixed your mind on accepting His answer. You have shaken off the chains of self, me and my. You have escaped from I want, I think and I know what's best for me to being willing to simply ask what do You have for me Lord. I'm ready to listen and follow. Next there is **Able** which means do I have what it takes to complete the mission? Can I follow through? Do I have the physical strength and mental fortitude? Is there anything at all standing in the way or holding me back? Is there anything that would keep me from walking into my destiny? Is there anyone that I may not be able to walk with or away from? Then there is **Ready** which refers to time. Can I do it today, at this very moment. If the phone rang with the call I've been waiting for. If the letter came today or there was that knock at the door right now... Sure, I've been hoping and praying for a breakthrough moment but am I ready for it to happen? Have I prepared for it or have I spent a lot of time just talking about it? Now think of the heroes, the prophets, the leaders that you read about and consider some that may have been **willing** but not **ready**, ready but not **able**. There are many combinations for positive results or unrealized goals and there may be something standing between you and that breakthrough. Prepare us for WAR.

"Father God, thank you for another day of possibility. I have read your Word and I believe. Jehovah, I choose you as my God. You know my heart and desires. You have given me talents and a purpose for my life. I have tried different things but I have never really been fulfilled or at peace. I feel and know in my inner soul that there is something special for me to do. You have shown me the way that is right and you have protected me from the way that ends in destruction so it must be for a reason. It is my desire to serve you so please help me prepare for WAR. Help me to be Willing, Able and Ready. I claim your promises for that breakthrough for myself and for the others who are praying for one as well. Thanking you in advance for your answers and blessings. In Jesus' name, Amen."

In Matthew 9:9 Jesus said to Matthew, "Follow Me. And he arose, and followed Him." Hold On today and remember these words from Matthew that tell us how to be ready for WAR. **Willing** to answer the call and offer your all. **Able** to stand and walk with Jesus and **Ready** to start the journey right then and there. Today, is a great day, for WAR.

HoldOn 2 Overcome. H2O.

No Wrong Numbers

How many times have you dialed a wrong number? Today with the modern technologies of smartphones, contacts lists, autodial and even voice dialing you would think that there would be less wrong numbers being connected. Yet I get those calls pretty often and have to give the caller the sad news that they've reached the wrong number. Let's imagine for a moment that our prayers are phone calls to heaven and there is no wrong number. Matter of fact there isn't even a specific number of digits, any magical code words or anything special needed for a call to heaven. Just think about Him. Just call His name in your mind and you will get a hello from the switchboard at the throne of God. He says hello and calls you by name because he was expecting your call.

"FATHER GOD, THANK YOU FOR THE DIRECT LINE AND YOUR PHONE book the Bible. I'm calling because I need to speak to you today. Lord, I've got some things that I can't handle but I believe you can. I'm just tired of trying and I'm sure tired of failing. Lord, I just want to get it right this time so I claim your promises in faith. I'm asking for your guidance and direction as I press forward today. I know that I am not the only one needing an answer so I ask for the power to pray blessings

on others as well. Let me be blessed enough to bless others. Show me the way so I can show others. I am calling on You Jesus because you have proven to be trustworthy, dependable and right on time. Please protect and keep me, heal and restore me and let this request also cover any and all those in need. I'm reaching out to you because only you know and only you can fulfill our needs. Now please forgive me and save me and I will give you all the praise and glory. In Jesus' name I claim it, Amen."

Hold On Family, 2 Chronicles 7:14 says that "if my people, which are called by my name, shall humble themselves and pray...then I will hear from heaven." That's all it takes. So call with confidence. Just dial 53787, that's "JESUS." Someone always answers and you will never get a busy signal or a wrong number.

So Pray On. PrayOn 2 Overcome. P2O.

The Hallelujah Pass

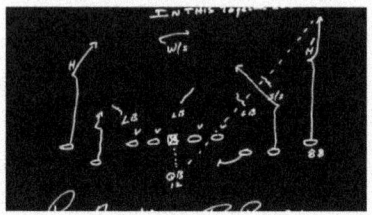

Have you ever heard of the Hail Mary Pass? Well if you've ever played a pickup game of football you've heard of one, seen one, thrown one and might even have caught one. It's the go-to solution for desperate situations. Now, imagine it's the big game and you're in the final minute of the fourth quarter and the clock is ticking. No field goal, touchback, or single point will do. We are down and pushed back to our own goal line. The only way to win this game is to score. You are the coach and you know there is only one play to ensure victory and so you call it in, the "Hail Jesus Pass." Send all the prayer receivers downfield, bow your head, close your eyes, and launch one into the stratosphere knowing it WILL be received in the end zone of the throne room.

"FATHER GOD, THANK YOU. LORD, PLEASE HEAR AND RECEIVE THIS plea from your child. My back is against the wall. There is no way out. Every option has been explored and I'm all out of chances. It is now or never. I need you right away. I claim the promise of your word that if I pray in Jesus name, asking in line with your will and offer you all the praise then I can be sure that you will answer me. I need a miracle Father God and I believe! I will wait now for your answer. I have done all that I can do and now I will not move, I will not turn, I will not go

forward or back until I hear from you my God. I place it in your hands, Amen."

Hold On Family, it is recorded in Mark 9:23 that Jesus Himself said "everything is possible for one who believes" and I still believe in last minute miracles. How about you? Well, hold on, hold on, hold on. Today is a great day for a Miracle. Can you hear it? The cheering in heaven. Your "Hail Jesus Pass" was received for a touchdown.

Now Hold on. HoldOn 2 Overcome. H2O.

No Accident Prayer

Look up on youtube. "His eye is on the sparrow" Lauryn Hill and Tanya Blount. http://youtu.be/_eAboY5zfYE

Can we really rap our minds around this big, omniscient, omnipresent, all knowing and powerful God? He keeps billions of universes with trillions of planets and stars dancing through time and space without them bumping into each other. With all the millions of people on this earth it can be hard to fathom that He has time for just one, me. God stays pretty busy and maybe that's why our prayer hasn't been answered yet. Maybe God has a full schedule or just didn't hear my prayer?

I had to pray this morning, *really pray*. I was completely honest with God and laid it all out there. Then I stood up, reached for my phone and when I pressed the power button the first thing I saw on the screen was this picture. Right there in bright red letters, "God heard you. Just be patient." Like a giant telescope in heaven that zoomed in on the earth, then to the United States, to this state, this city, this house, this one person kneeling here trying to hold it together for life itself and God said, "I heard you!" Someone had posted that picture on social media and they probably didn't know it but those words were just for me. God meant that message at that very moment for me and now I'm passing it on to you. You may be on your knees, really praying right now too. Hold on family and be assured, He has it all in control. He has me, you, her, him, them and it *all* in His sights. He isn't too busy to hear your prayers. Luke 15:7 "I tell you that in the same way there will be more rejoicing in heaven over *one* sinner who repents than over ninety-nine who do not need to repent. That's right, "one." He sees and hears every single one. Jesus came for one, He died for one, and He's coming back for one. That one is Me. Jesus is coming back for [say your name] and don't you forget it.

"Dear Lord, thank you for loving me just that much. Thank you for the reminders that you see me, you hear me and you haven't forgotten me. Now please be with me. Remind me again and again. Don't give up on me Lord. We've come too far together. Let today be the day that I know and feel your presence and grant me peace. Amen."

This message you are reading is no accident. It was meant for the one who needed it.

So please pass it on and Hold on. HoldOn 2 Overcome.

Game Time

When the football players walk onto the field as a team the goal is to *win* the game. Each individual has a part to play but the strategy for success is for the players to work together. The better they cooperate the more their success. It is a collective effort. Well Hold On Family, we are all in the game of life together. We are in the huddle when the coach calls in the big play...."PRAY!"

"Father God, first we always give thanks. We come today wanting so badly to win. So we are asking you Father to please show and guide us. Reveal it to us Lord. Please make it so plain that we can't miss what it is that You want us to do: which path, which words, which place, which person, which decision? Lord, what do I do? We need you to look into the future like only you can do and guide us now on the best path for us. We need healing, jobs, homes, protection, families funds and a whole list of other things. So we claim the promise of your word that you will supply all our needs. We lift up everyone today but especially that each one that reads this prayer will be given a clear message and revelation today. Show us the way to go and we will give you all the praise, honor and glory. In Jesus' name we claim it, Amen."

Now jog out onto that field called life with confidence. James

5:16 tells us to "confess your faults one to another, and pray one for another, that ye may be healed. The effectual fervent prayer of a righteous man availeth much." Availeth much...translation is you win!

Now Hold On. HoldOn 2 Overcome. H2O.

Do You Recognize?

Exodus 16:14-15 records the first day that the manna fell. "When the dew was gone, thin flakes like frost on the ground appeared on the desert floor. When the Israelites saw it, they said to each other, "What is it?" For they did not know what it was. Moses said to them, "It is the bread the Lord has given you to eat." Hold on Family, that first appearance of this stuff called "manna" was actually an answer to their prayers. Exodus 16:3 records their request which was actually more of a complaint. "The Israelites said to them, "If only we had died by the Lord's hand in Egypt! There we sat around pots of meat and ate all the food we wanted, but you have brought us out into this desert to starve this entire assembly to death." Then verse 4 gives God's answer. "Then the Lord said to Moses, I will rain down bread from heaven for you."

Family, God does answer prayers! Even if we don't recognize it or know what to do with it. So today, take a few moments to look around you and ask yourself has God already answered my prayer but I didn't recognize it? Remember Jeremiah 33:3 says "Call to me and I will answer you and tell you great and unsearchable things you do not know." Family, when we pray we also need to remember to pray for recognition. God's ways are not our ways so we may need clarification and revelation for our prayers. Don't miss the blessing. You better recognize.

"LORD, THANK YOU FOR HEARING AND ANSWERING OUR PRAYERS. *Please give us wisdom and discernment. We claim the words of 2 Kings 6:16,17 and ask that you open our eyes to see your mighty works around us. Show us that you are with us and you are greater than anyone or anything that could ever come against us. Let us feel your presence and be assured. Remind someone today that all things are working for them and today is not the day to consider giving up or in. Give us strength to fight our battles and the compassion to help someone else who may be struggling. For every breakthrough and every blessing we give you all the praise Jesus, Amen."*

Remember Balaalm (Number 22)? The answer you've been hoping for just might be right in front of you. Maybe not in the way you expected, but it's the answer just the same. Recognize.

HOLD ON. HOLDON 2 OVERCOME. H2O

Where There's Smoke

There is this saying, "Where there's smoke, there's fire." In Exodus 19 Moses is attempting to lead God's chosen people from Egypt to the Promised Land. They have all recently witnessed miraculous signs and great wonders and while most of the people are confident a great number of them are still unsure why they are even in a desert. We can imagine that some are just following the crowd or doing what their parents did and some probably don't have a clue and are just going through the motions but as with any group of people there are some unhappy, never satisfied, always complaining detractors. They are stubborn and in outright defiance of God. Family, the truth today is that God is trying to lead you somewhere, specifically to the promised land. There is a message for us all found in Exodus 19:16 "On the morning of the third day there was thunder and lightning, with a thick cloud over the mountain, and a very loud trumpet blast. Everyone in the camp trembled. Mount Sinai was covered with smoke because the Lord descended on it in fire." Family, just remember this. Where there's smoke there is fire and that fire is Jesus. The smoke is a sign that He is with you.

. . .

"*Father God, we humbly give thanks for this living Word that still speaks to us today. Now we come Lord like those people at the mountain that day needing to hear from our God. Lord could you show us the smoke and let us hear the trumpets to assure us that you are near. We call out to you as your children to claim the same promises you said you would fulfill that day on that mountain. Father, please free us with mighty miracles. Father, please guide us through dangers seen and unseen. Lead us, ever-present by night and day. Feed us, supply for us, deliver us and protect us from the approaching armies seeking to return us to bondage and Lord as we step forward in faith today please take us through to the Promised Land. Now we kneel at the mountain believing that where we see smoke, we know you are there with us. In the name of Jesus we claim it, Amen.*"

Hold on and pray. Don't you dare give up now. What's happening around us should actually confirm that what He said was true. He's brought us this far and He will carry us through.

HOLD ON AND SEE THE SMOKE. HOLDON 2 OVERCOME. H2O

MIRACL1

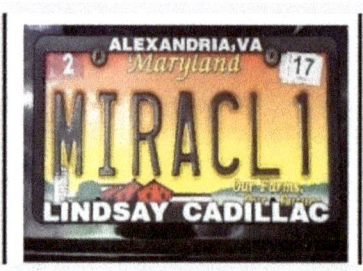

I turned around after taking the picture of this license plate to see two gentlemen coming my way. One of them asked me why I had taken a picture of his car? The truth would surely put them at ease so I shared that I collect pictures of tags with positive and spiritual messages. I was happy to pull up the photo gallery on my phone and share some of my collection with them. Honestly there was a change in the atmosphere and an electric tingle of anticipation as I saw the men's eyes twinkle. The other man said "Well, it's my wife's car and she *is* a living miracle. The doctors said she was going to die back in 2003 and she's still alive here in 2015." (Cue the organ!) Hold on Family, do you think God did his last miracle in 2003? Does He not have more breakthroughs in His storehouse? Was **MIRACL1** the only one or can God make me **MIRACL2**? The answer is YES! His miracles are innumerable and without limit.

"*FATHER GOD, WE COME THANKING YOU FOR THE REMINDERS EVEN ON license plates. Somebody, right now, writing and reading this needs a **MIRACL2**. Even Me Father God, let some drops now fall on me. You know the situations, the problems, the deadlines, the diagnosis. Father, according to your word you are the only God that knows the* *future and can make it come to pass. So we ask according to your promises that today you perform a miracle for ME.* Whatever number it is Lord please let there be one today for ME. *In the name of Jesus I claim the answer, Amen."*

He Promised, so keep claiming it and maybe design your own personal license plate to tell the world the story. He promised miracles. Plural, innumerable, unlimited, and beyond what any man can even imagine and today is a great day for my number to be called.

HOLD ON. HOLD ON. HOLDON 4 YOUR MIRACLE.

Just Did It

What's a good way to explain why you refuse to quit praying? What's a word for it? What do you tell people when they ask you about why you are still praying after all this time? You could say that you believe praying encourages the person or prayer defeats the enemy. Perhaps praying lets you feel closer to God and not because every prayer is answered immediately with the desired result. Sometimes, especially when you are struggling with a particular situation, just being able to utter a prayer is a victory in itself. Praying when you don't want to pray *is* the victory and that's what God wants. He wants us to come and talk with Him all the time and for every circumstance as long as we are hoping, seeking, yearning and reaching. Everyday that we keep praying, we have the VICTORY! As long as we did it (pray), we have (overcome). So just do it.

"FATHER GOD, WE JUST HAVE TO SAY THANK YOU AND BELIEVE THAT *these words in themselves are nails in the enemy's coffin. No matter what he tries to throw at us we can and will still pray. We will call your name above all names, true and living God, that has answered so many times before. Lord, you know our many struggles, attacks, diseases and unanswered prayers but yet still we will call on you Lord.*

We will repeat the promises of your Word that you will answer and show us great and mighty things. So please accept these words from our hearts to yours. In the name of Jesus. Amen."

Just keep praying and Hold On. We are already victorious today because we just did it!

Spread the word and HoldOn 2 Overcome. H2O

Theories

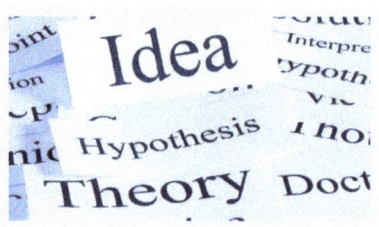

Someone shared a theory that they had heard in conversation and it went something like this. Jesus died every time He healed someone. In order to heal, He had to give His own life. Well, it may sound good but I'll offer a counter proposal. God, my God *is* life and continually creates and produces more of life. Imagine a glass full of water sitting under a dripping faucet. For every drip that spills over it is immediately replaced by another from the faucet above. That describes God. He IS life, love and hope. He is the faucet and the glass. He is forever full and ready to overflow so that whatever love He sends out is simultaneously replenished by the love that He produces. In Mark 5:30 and Luke 8:46 Jesus asked "who touched me because I felt power/love/life flow out of me." Hold on Family, God is endless and that is our hope. He will never run out of what we need. His resources never diminish or dissipate, they are only transferred. He says "I AM the alpha, omega, beginning and end. Always was and always will be. Just by being God He is constantly and continually procreating more of Himself. So for every drop that He bestows on us another has already taken its place and is ready for our prayer request to release it. Today, we can still access those same healing powers by touching the hem of Christ's garments. He is alive and all we have to do is pray.

. . .

"Dear Lord, the first words will always be thank you. For Your Word and this incredible account of how a person was and still can be healed by even the slightest contact with you. So we come pressing close and reaching out for the hem of your garment. For those that need physical healing we ask that you do what no one else can do for them. Strengthen them to endure the trial knowing that they are being a blessing to others. Take this opportunity to show the professionals who you are and what only you can do. Please relieve the discomfort people are feeling in their bodies and in their minds. We are expecting a complete restoration of health because we ask it in the name of the one who laid down His life, so that we might live. Amen."

That's my theory and I'm sticking with it. Now Hold On, HoldOn 2 Overcome.

Hold on today. HoldOn 2 Overcome. H2O

Spoiled Rotten

"**D**addy I Want!" Maybe you remember the story about Willy Wonka and the Chocolate Factory. There was this scene where everyone on the screen moaned and everyone watching groaned because of this one little girl's obscene level of brattitude. Everyone asked what kind of parent is her father? Hold On a moment and think of your prayers. How many of your prayers fall under the category, "Daddy, I want...!" What do you think of a child who only comes to talk to their parent when they want something? What about that friend or family member whose entire conversation is about what you could do for them? Don't we all know someone that just feels they are entitled to whatever they want? What kind of relationship do you have with the person that feels they are entitled? Well, considering some of the prayers that we offer to God we could imagine that He could feel the same way about us but He doesn't. He still accepts every prayer.

*"F*ATHER, SOMETIMES IT'S HARD TO IMAGINE HOW AND WHY YOU LOVE *us so much? Why did you create us if you can really see the future? If you knew that Adam and Eve would fall and you'd have to allow a flood that would almost wipe everyone off the face of the earth. If you*

knew you'd have to come yourself and give your life to save ours. If you knew that even after all that we would still not believe, we would choose other gods and then become spoiled, rotten, brats coming to beg you over and over again for junk that doesn't even matter. The only way I can imagine it is to imagine the love a parent has for their child. A parent loves their child unconditionally and without measure. Thank you Jesus for allowing me to be your child. Now please forgive me for all my brattitude and help me to mature into the person you can use for your good and glory. Take my desires and align them with your will. This is my prayer in the name of Jesus, Amen."

What God?

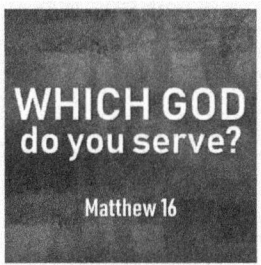

The word "God" has become generic. Amazing sometimes to hear that word come out of some people's mouths directly after they were spewing an encyclopedia's worth of profanity and vulgarity. Some of the worst people living some of the worst lifestyles almost without emotion "thank God" for allowing them to be such degenerates. How can you go against God and then thank God at the same time? I think we need some clarification. I think we might need to ask what *God* are you referring to? There are many gods. I am told that there are more than 500 million gods in Hinduism alone. I think that if we are going to talk about a god we will first need to qualify what god it is we are referring to? If we are going to give God credit, first establish which god is worthy. If we are going to visit "God's house" shouldn't we ask who is honored and worshiped there? So if someone is going to pray to god or in the name of god, shouldn't we at least specify who that god is? Surely we want to pray to a god that can answer, right?

"FATHER GOD, CREATOR OF ME AND ALL THINGS EVERYWHERE. GOD *of heaven and earth. Born in a manger, healer and teacher. Forgiver of guilt. The God that knows the future because He is in the future and then brings that future to be present. The God that has power in the mention of His name. The God that gives hope. The God who gave us His living word to speak to all men, at all times, in all places. The God of Abraham, Isaac and Jacob. The God that walks in fiery furnaces and shuts lion's months. The God that does miracles, heals the sick and feeds the hungry. The God that demons run from and sinners can turn to. The God who left His throne in glory to come to the dirty earth and allow Himself to be Crucified so that I wouldn't have to be. The God that death couldn't hold in the grave. The God that was resurrected and went back to the heavenly courts to prepare a place for me to come and live with Him one day soon. What God? THAT GOD! The God that listens to my moans and groans then sends me an answer that only He could know. To the one and only God that the winds and rain obeys, Jehovah I chose to worship you and now in the words of Elijah I ask you to show us all this day who is the true and living God, Amen.*

Isn't it good to serve a living God that hears and answers prayers? Just try Him. Ask Him something, something special, a secret, that only you and He will know from the privacy of your mind. Then when He answers, you will know it had to be Him. That's how He reveals Himself. The true God, answers. Send your requests, but be specific with the address. Not all who are called God can answer but mine, my God can!

SO I HOLD ON. HOLDON 2 OVERCOME.

In the News

Could you imagine Ghandi or Mother Theressa watching your local news broadcast? What would Martin Luther King Jr. say about today's headlines? What do you think your great grandparents would think if they were alive today? Surely there would be a lot of gasping, head shaking and quite possibly tears. Is this the future they imagined, talked about and sacrificed for? Nowadays the news can be downright depressing as people grow increasingly numb to crime and violence. But did you ever think of praying for a news story or for those involved in a story? Do we need to know the people personally to pray for them? Ecclesiastes 8:6,7 says "For there is a proper time and procedure for *every* matter, though a person may be weighed down by misery. Since no one knows the future, who can tell someone else what is to come?" In other words, since we don't know what is to come, we can pray for a change in any situation. Whatever the Breaking News, whenever the headline appears or wherever the reporters gather, we can pray.

"FATHER GOD, WE THANK YOU FOR KEEPING US YET ANOTHER WEEK IN *this crazy world with all the crazy news. For every victory, every step of progress and every rescue we say thank you. We come to place our concerns and needs at your throne understanding that none of it is a surprise to you Lord. Please help us to make sense of it all when it doesn't make sense. Father, we lift the immediate needs that require answers in the next few hours and the situations that we have been praying about for a long time. We are your children and because we believe in you please work a news-worthy miracle for each person gathered here. We've heard the reports but we are not shaken nor afraid. The stories are gloomy but we are hopeful. The news tells us that we need a breakthrough and we know that breakthroughs are your specialty. We've brought it to you Lord. We give it all to you Lord. Now please surround us with your presence and your peace so that we don't have to worry about what's on the news anymore. Instead please show us the positivity and the hope we have when we claim the promises of your Good News. In Jesus' name we pray, Amen."*

No matter what the report, outlook, diagnosis, prognosis or situation, always remember to pray.

THEN PRAY SOME MORE AND HOLD ON. HOLDON 2 OVERCOME. H2O

Hammer

I magine you are a carpenter working on a construction site. If a hammer just fell from the sky right in front of you, what would you do? I think first I'd say thank you Jesus because it didn't hit me in the head but then there would be some decisions to make. Clearly a hammer would be a useful tool but most tools only have one job. Saws have one edge that cut. Drills only do one thing; they make holes. A hammer has two ends and remarkably has two purposes. One end of a hammer is round and flattened for pounding things in but the other end is a forked claw for pulling things out. They are equally useful but opposite functions. So you could pick up that hammer and get busy pounding with great motivation and self-determination or you could pick it up and start pulling, ripping and removing.

Hold on a minute, did you forget something? Did you remember to pray before making your decision? Did you stop and seek God's guidance for His purpose? If He sent the hammer shouldn't you find out what He wants you to do with it and if He didn't send it wouldn't you want to know that He doesn't want you to touch it at all? For the answers to our prayers shouldn't we consult the one who can answer?

. . .

"*FATHER GOD, I THANK YOU FOR KEEPING ME SAFE FROM ABOVE, beneath and all around. I'm coming to you now Lord asking you to show me your purpose for my day, my week and my entire life. Father, please strengthen my faith and patience to wait for your directions for everything I do. Please see my future and guide me to my best outcomes. Father I pray not just for my personal benefit but I'm asking to be blessed so that I can and will be a blessing to others. Father because I ask please heal somebody, free somebody, answer somebody, relieve somebody, comfort somebody, feed somebody and please use me to save somebody. I claim the promise of your own words that you will answer me if I seek your will and ask in the name of Jesus, Amen.*"

Hold on and pray without ceasing. 1 Thessalonians 5:16-18 says,"Rejoice always. Pray continually. Give thanks in *all* circumstances; for this is God's will for you in Christ Jesus." He made it. He sent it and He knows what He wants you to do with it. He made you. He will send you and He will tell you what He wants you to do when you get there. He knows best how to use hammers and you.

SO HOLD ON FOR HIS ANSWERS. HOLD ON. HOLDON 2 OVERCOME. H2O

A.P.R.

I was driving and something suddenly flew toward the windshield of my car. Caught off guard our defense mechanisms automatically spring into action. Most people would blink, close their eyes, even duck their heads thinking they may be hit. It happens so fast that your body instinctively reacts. Your heart races and your mind speeds ahead but what if this moment really was going to be your last moment alive? If you had a choice wouldn't you want one last moment to pray? Maybe it would be a good idea to practice our defense mechanisms and incorporate an **A.P.R.** or the "**Automatic Prayer Response.**"

Pretty amazing actually when you think about how many people when faced with sudden danger utter the words, "Oh God!" Amazing that there is an autonomic response designed and coded into every human being to recognize and praise their creator. Philippians 2:10-11 says "that at the name of Jesus, every knee should bow...and that every tongue should confess that Jesus Christ is Lord, to the glory of God the Father." Romans 14:11 says "For it is written, As I live, saith the Lord, every knee shall bow to me, and every tongue shall confess to God." I say it would be a good idea to start practicing our A.P.R. so when the time comes to use it, calling the name of Jesus will be automatic and instinctive.

. . .

"THANK YOU LORD. I BELIEVE THAT YOU ARE GOD AND THE CREATOR *of heaven and earth. I believe you cannot lie, cannot fail and your Word cannot return void. So I ask you to go with me and protect me wherever I am. Lord please remind me to make my first and last words all day and every day "Jesus." In His name I ask you to forgive me for everything I have ever done that is not pleasing to you and save me when you come in the clouds of glory, Amen."*

Hold On, now you have implemented your A.P.R. Keep pressing and always remember that even when we don't expect it He is still there. Our A.P.R. is evidence to the fact that all we have to do is Hold On because today is a great day for my miracle.

SO HOLDON 2 OVERCOME. H2O

The Lifted

I was feeling the pressure and sometimes it can seem like tons. Then my phone rang and it was someone on the other line that just offered to pray for me. Nothing fancy or creative, just an earnest request directly to the Father on my behalf to do something to help me. The phone call ended and I actually did feel a little... lighter. The more I thought about it the lighter I felt. Later on in the week things again became a little intense but I felt a certain calm, that familiar lightness. Suddenly it just came to my mind. I bet somebody is praying for me. Right now, at this very moment, someone is lifting me up and I feel it.

Hold on Family, have you ever felt lifted? Recently I was deeply contemplating Matthew 18:20 "For where two or three are gathered together in my name, there I am in the midst of them." But why did it say two or three? Three would include two, right? There must be some significance. What came to me was that the two is your private prayer. You and God in the car, the closet, your private prayer wherever you are but the 3, that's the social prayer when it's You, God and another person all in agreement. Therefore even when it appears for all practical purposes to just be two people praying together there are actually three present. The truth is we never actually pray alone. Matthew promises us that Jesus is right there with us. (Praise break) So hold on and keep praying. Even one makes two. Hold on and know that you are not alone today and I am praying for you. I am praying now for everyone that will ever read these words.

"Father God, thank you. I pray that each and every person that ever reads these words will know that they are not alone and be blessed because of this prayer. I pray they feel the lifting and the lightness that comes along with the presence of angels. I pray that you reveal yourself to them wherever they are. I pray that their minds grasp the intentional purpose and timing of them reading these words right now. Somebody needed to know that you are real today Lord. Somebody needed a sign. Somebody asked for a signal and here is the evidence that you saw them in the future and sent these words to speak to their heart at this moment. Now help us to pass on the blessing and the breakthrough. For all those praying all around this world I claim it in the name of Jesus, Amen."

Can you feel it? Good. Remember that you are never alone in prayer. Now, go lift somebody else and Hold On.

HoldOn 2 Overcome. H2O

The Peace

Peace. I desire peace. I often pray for peace but what does it really mean? To hold your peace. Go in peace. Live in peace. Just ask yourself, do I have peace? When was the last time I experienced peace? What is blocking my peace? Am I praying for peace? Hold on Family, I offer a few words from the Word. Leviticus 26:6 says "And I will give peace in the land, and ye shall lie down, and none shall make you afraid: and I will rid evil beasts out of the land, neither shall the sword go through your land. In Judges 6:23 " the LORD said unto him, peace be unto thee; fear not: thou shalt not die." 1 Samuel 1:17 says to "Go in peace, and may the God of Israel grant you what you have asked of him." Psalms 4:8 "I will both lay me down in peace and sleep: for thou, Lord, only makest me dwell in safety. Isaiah 26:3 "Thou wilt keep him in perfect peace, whose mind is stayed on thee: because he trusteth in thee." Aha. Peace seems to be living without fear and in safety. Rest, lying down, sleeping while not even being concerned about life itself. That sounds wonderful. I propose that if you don't have peace today, pray and ask for it. It really is just that simple.

. . .

"Father God, thank you for allowing us to come and ask for peace. We also ask that you strengthen our faith and trust in you. Now I pray that you will bring your presence, your power and your love to the person reading these words right now. I am asking you Jesus to declare in their life today that same command you gave to the storm that day on the sea of Galilee, "peace, be still." I pray that you take away their fear and provide them safety. I ask that you allow them to rest and even go to sleep without worrying about anything that has been on their mind. Take away the thoughts and replace the concerns with sweet dreams of heaven and thee. In the mighty name of Jesus we claim it done and give you praise, honor and glory for your peace. Amen."

Hold on and live, work and pray for peace. Today is a great day, for my miracle.

Just Hold on 2 peace, Peace 2 Overcome. P2O.

Unspoken

They call them testimony services. People come together in a group and share their stories, their triumphs and their prayers. The prayer requests can be as different as night and day, sometimes only one and other times a long list of things. Inevitably someone will raise their hand, stand up and then just say this one word, "unspoken." As a youngster I may not have fully understood but now as an adult I realize that some personal things aren't for everybody to hear. You shouldn't put all your business in the street. So there are the unspoken requests when someone wants to avoid the judgmental looks or suspicious stares. When you may be carrying a burden that you can't even mention without unleashing a flood of emotions and tears. When you can't say it, it's unspoken and that means just say my name to Jesus. So today we will ask for prayer requests and we will ask the God who knows and sees all to especially move on the behalf of the unspoken.

"FATHER GOD, WE COME TODAY TO THANK YOU FOR JUST LETTING US come. We must acknowledge that you brought us through another week and even if we did nothing but lay in the bed all day we still give you praise for keeping our hearts beating and the roof from collapsing on top of us. We thank you for the ability to request things from you

through this method called prayer and for the answers reminding us that somebody hears and answers.

Now Father God we have some specific needs like the tests, the appointments, the treatments and surgeries that are scheduled. We pray especially for those fighting against the enemies of cancer and that someone reading this prayer will be healed because we claimed it. There are resumes being revised, interviews, hirings and firings but you already know we need to pay our bills and keep food on our tables.There are utilities and tuition, transportation and retirements to plan for. Father, we pray for wisdom and direction with our resources. We pray for the spirit of generosity to remind us to be a blessing to others even when we don't have a lot ourselves. Father we offer a special prayer for families knowing the enemy seeks to kill and destroy and targets the strength of togetherness. For our children, Lord keep them. We pray for the unspoken prayers. For those who are barely Holding on. For those who can't see or feel you. For those who feel darkness and have been struggling for months and even years. For those going it alone and those who worry about letting go. For those carrying the burdens of others as their cross. For those that know it will take a miracle but are faithful to pray and ask for it. Father God we pray that you take the unspoken prayers, translate them into heavenly petitions and answer them all today. Relieve the pressure, heal the wounds, take away the pain and restore their faith. This we claim in the name of Jesus and thanking you already for what you are about to do, Amen."

Now, Hold on and believe that heaven heard and heaven heals, even the unspoken.

HoldOn 2 Overcome. H2O.

Jesus Fuel

It's one thing to see that needle point to empty but to run out of gas while driving is definitely an even more scary and unpleasant situation. But have you ever felt empty? No really, completely empty? When you've tried your best and given it all you have to give. When you can't even care any more. No energy, no hope, little faith, can't cope. Cloudy days and sleepless nights, don't care to talk, don't care to fight. When your inner gauge is on empty and you are literally running on fumes? It's at these times that we need to pull into the station of prayer. We need a fill up of Jesus Fuel. Let's pray.

LORD, I WANT TO SAY THANK YOU AGAIN FOR THOSE THINGS I USUALLY give thanks for like life, waking us this morning, food and shelter but Father today I come to you to be honest and tell you that I am weary from the battles and I just don't know what to do. You invited us in your word to come to you, to test you, to prove you. I know that I am not the only one to ever need answers. Gideon, Moses, Abraham and even Jesus Himself had to plead for direction and strength so Lord I too am coming now asking for a miraculous sign. God, I have been running on empty but still trying to Hold On to faith. Even while I was praying and fasting, waiting and believing the situations have gotten even worse. You said the water wouldn't cover me and the fire wouldn't burn me but Lord honestly I feel like I'm drowning and burning at the same time. I have run out of fuel and the enemy is attacking so I need you now to fight this battle for me like you said you would.

Do you hear me Father? Are you really there? What am I doing wrong? What direction do I need to take? Father, I want to serve and represent you. I want to believe but right now I just can't see my way through. Lord, you said you'd come for one and right now there are many of us, reading this message, that know they are losing the fight of faith. Lord, I don't want to be disrespectful but it's a fact that I am struggling and my hope has faded. I don't want to read. I can barely find energy to pray.

Father God, you've got to come through for me. I know there is no other, no place, no thing that can do it and so I'm crying out to you. Please Jesus, FILL ME. Jesus, come lift me up. Jesus, come calm me down. Jesus, come assure me. Jesus, please come take care of these bills. Jesus, come put an end to this attack. Jesus, come give me strength for this surgery/treatment/procedure and heal me completely. Jesus, let me sleep at night. Jesus, lead me to the right job. Jesus, provide a roof over my head. Jesus, send us someone to love and be loved by. Jesus, lift my head from shame and restore my reputation. Jesus, break this addiction. Lord, I need an answer today and please make a way. Please fill me up again so that I can continue my journey and fulfill my purpose and I will give you all the praise, honor, and glory. In Jesus's name, Amen. H2O.

This message was intentionally placed at the end of this book. While it is our goal to be inspiring and encouraging we want everyone to know that we do understand that there are those dark times. Those times when we literally can not even pray. There will be times when we don't want to turn on the lights or open any windows. We don't make calls, take calls or go to the door. There is a place called empty and we will all reserve a room at one time or another there and that's OK. He's still there, still watching, still listening. Just imagine Him standing there next to a gas pump with a hose and nozzle in His hand. He knows what to do. Just stand still for a moment…

H2O

Afterword

The end of these pages is not the end of this journey. As long as there's need to hold on there will be more hold on messages. Until that time you can always go to holdon2overcome.com for more inspiration as we make continuous updates.

Also by W. Patrick Harris

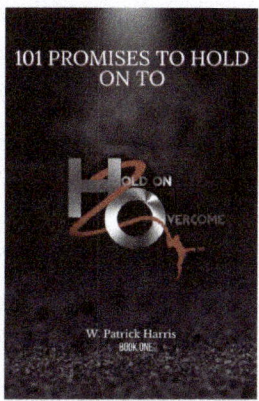

These messages aren't necessarily for entertainment or casual reading. No, these messages are born of a struggle and presented to you here to fuel determination, faith, and HOPE. If you're looking for a quick minute-devotional while you sip a morning beverage, this may not be the place for you.

But if you're standing on the ledge of a building or balancing on the side of a bridge looking down into murky depths. For those who are considering giving up or feel all hope is lost. Financial Problems, Separations, Divorce, Pain, Sickness. Everyone at some time or another has experienced some form of distress or trauma. Unemployment, Disease, Lies and Slander, Wayward children, Deadlines, Aging parents, Grief and Loss, Loneliness, Foreclosures, Dependency and Addictions, Lost Loves, Lives, and Unfulfilled Dreams. The weariness of struggling for such a long time you're down, but not out. HOLD ON!

101 Promises. 101 Strategies. 101 Encouragements. 101 Breakthroughs. One of them is for you.

www.ingramcontent.com/pod-product-compliance
Lightning Source LLC
Chambersburg PA
CBHW062021290426
44108CB00024B/2736